MORE JESUS
LESS RELIGION

MORE JESUS
LESS RELIGION

Moving *from* Rules to Relationship

Stephen Arterburn Coauthor of *Every Man's Battle*
& Jack Felton

WATERBROOK
PRESS

MORE JESUS, LESS RELIGION
PUBLISHED BY WATERBROOK PRESS
12265 Oracle Blvd., Suite 200
Colorado Springs, Colorado 80921
A division of Random House, Inc.

ISBN 1-57856-250-3

Published in association with the literary agency of Alive Communications, Inc., 7680 Goddard Street, Suite 200, Colorado Springs, Colorado 80920, www.alivecommunications.com

Library of Congress Cataloging-in-Publication Data
Arterburn, Stephen, 1953-
    More Jesus, less religion : moving from rules to relationship / Stephen Arterburn and Jack Felton.— 1st ed.
        p. cm.
    ISBN 1-57856-250-3 (pbk.)
        1. Faith.   I. Felton, Jack.   II. Title
BV4637.A685 2000
231.7—dc21
                                                                99-055258

Printed in the United States of America
2006

10 9

This book is dedicated to Dick Ragsdale.
Rare is the person who has a mentor and encourager
full of wisdom, insight, and godly character.
Dick Ragsdale has been this for me.
Above his business acumen he is a loving husband,
a dedicated father, and an extremely proud grandfather.
Thank you, Dick, for all you are
and all you have done for me and my family.
—S.A.

———————

This book is dedicated to my son, Jack, the "Iceman,"
my daughter, Christy,
and my wife, Robin, who keeps us all together.
—J.F.

CONTENTS

Acknowledgments

Thanks to Dan Rich, publisher of WaterBrook, who allowed us to provide this follow-up to *Toxic Faith*. To Laura Barker, managing editor, and the whole WaterBrook team: You are a dream publisher.

Special thanks for the editorial talent of Steve Halliday and Larry Libby. You turned our points of truth into a book of hope.

And sincere gratitude to Greg Johnson, who saw the project through as super agent and friend.

A DIFFERENT WAY OF OPERATING

I have published thirty books in my writing career. Some have been best-sellers; others worst sellers. But of all the projects I've done, by far the most rewarding has been *Toxic Faith* (later printed in paperback under the title *Faith That Hurts, Faith That Heals*).

Just last weekend I was in Orlando among eighteen thousand women at a Women of Faith conference, a movement I was privileged to help create. But the only book of mine I heard anyone mention was *Toxic Faith*. One woman repeated something I've heard many times: "That book saved my life and my marriage, and it rescued me from a very unhealthy church where I felt trapped."

I'm so grateful that God helped me see that not everything about a church that makes us uncomfortable is "our problem." Sometimes it's the church's problem. Now, don't get me wrong. I deeply believe in church and I attend a very healthy, strong congregation about which I'll say more later. I believe God is doing a great work today in churches. But many times people never stop to think about whether their church builds them up or tears them down, whether it frees them to enjoy a loving relationship with God through Jesus or whether it's hampering and destroying that relationship.

Toxic Faith was primarily about unhealthy beliefs and what we need to do to identify and move beyond toxic faith systems. *More Jesus, Less Religion* picks up where *Toxic Faith* left off. In the former book we spent only one chapter, the final one, talking about healthy faith; in this book we'll spend most of our time describing it.

It has become obvious to me since writing *Toxic Faith* that the way Jesus did things on this earth was so different from how many of us operate. Often we act in ways to make us feel good about ourselves or to support a tradition we've adopted or to uphold some cherished rule. But Jesus always valued relationships over rules. Whether it was healing a person on the Sabbath or sharing a meal with a known "sinner," Jesus acted in unpredictable, unexpected, and life-changing ways. And the fact is, wherever the Master traveled and ministered, two things inevitably happened: People's lives were changed and the established religious order was upset.

The most opposition Jesus encountered was not from sinners caught in horrible sins, but from the religious leaders who saw him as a threat to their power, position, and authority. Jesus tended to devalue human systems and rituals because they induced people to lose their first love. Men and women captive to such toxic systems focused on their own power, rather than on the power of God. And when they did think of God, they distorted his image. These people knew God only as a binder of lives, as a vindictive, angry Creator. It took the life and death of Jesus to reposition the image of God in the minds and hearts of desperate men and women. Through Christ they saw God's compassion, love, and grace.

Today, the toughest opposition to Christianity comes from what I would call legalists. Like the Pharisees, legalists are so caught up in tradition that they fail to see that mercy and grace are every bit as important as discipline and sacrifice.

Jesus used a verse from Hosea that I believe tears away the substructure of the legalist position. In this text our Savior lays the foundation of a healthy faith. In Hosea 6:6 the Lord declares, "I desire mercy, not sacrifice."

Relationships, not rules, should take precedence in our lives. Love, not legalism, must reign. Many legalists in our own day, just like the Pharisees, don't think they should hang around "evil people." They think they should avoid them and thus avoid being contaminated. But the church today, just as Jesus did, must get beyond stained glass and gates and walls and get into the community and be light where it is so urgently needed.

Jesus was so authentic and real that the masses were naturally drawn to him. Unholy people flocked to him—people you would never imagine wanting to be in the presence of God. Because of who he was and how he ministered, they crowded the hillsides and jostled each other on the lakeshores just to be near him. As Luke tells us, "The tax collectors and 'sinners' were all gathering around to hear him" (15:1).

What those tax gatherers and sinners needed, we still need today. We don't need more religion; what we need, *what we must have,* is more of Jesus. As commentator Terry C. Muck has written: "Counterfeit spiritualities do not work. But their persistent growth and appeal should teach us two important lessons. First, human beings created for fellowship with God abhor a spiritual vacuum. And second, only the real thing will effectively scratch the spiritual itch."[1]

We know that some who pick up this book might be offended by our assertion that we need "less religion" in our lives. In fact, when *Toxic Faith* was first released, some rejected the book on the assumption that we were "bashing the church." In reality, our book lifted up the Lord by seeking to build healthy churches and point people toward such fellowships. The only churches we bashed then (and still bash today) are those that have lost their first love, their passion for the One for whom the church exists.

It was Karl Marx who said, "Religion...is the opiate of the people." Religion, with all its rituals and trappings, can indeed be hypnotic. When all you do is jump through hoops to try to get to God, it is easy to either give up or to get weird trying to earn God's favor.

But if religion is a drug of the people, then a relationship with an all-loving God can keep each person truly full of life. Only when a relationship with God transcends all religious trappings does true fulfillment come. Religion and striving will not fulfill the empty places in our hearts. They will only dull the emptiness like a drug. It is only in a pure relationship with God that forgiveness can be experienced—and it is then no longer necessary to continue to run from pain. Jesus loves us wholly and forgives us completely. No drug can offer that!

I'm grateful that Jack Felton has once again joined me to help in writing this book, as he did almost a decade ago with *Toxic Faith*. Whenever the stories or anecdotes we use in *More Jesus, Less Religion* come from his experience, his name will appear in brackets, as in "I [Jack] have a son..." Otherwise, the experiences relayed are my own.

While toxic faith of whatever stripe will always appeal to tradition and established religion, healthy faith will always appeal to those who want to know the true and living God. To that end Jack and I write this book, focused more on Jesus and less on religion. Our ultimate goal is that, by reading this, you will grow in your relationship with Jesus and you will come to know that his love really is unconditional, that his yoke really is easy, and that his burden really is light.

And then you will have discovered the essence of healthy faith.

—Stephen Arterburn

CHAPTER 1

THE WAY THINGS ARE

A Healthy Faith Is Based in Reality

Have nothing to do with godless myths and old wives' tales; rather, train
yourself to be godly.

1 Timothy 4:7

David wrote, "Even though I walk through the valley of the shadow of death,
I will fear no evil, for you are with me" (Psalm 23:4).

That's the expression and expectation of a healthy faith. Not only that
God's presence will go with us, but that there are some dark, deadly, shadowed places on this old planet of ours. The valley of the shadow of death
exists in this world. I have seen it. So have you. It exists because we live in a
fallen world. A healthy faith gets us through that dark valley. Unhealthy faith
makes us pretend the valley doesn't even exist!

The same David also penned these words:

> For troubles without number surround me;
> > my sins have overtaken me, and I cannot see.
> They are more than the hairs of my head,
> > and my heart fails within me. (Psalm 40:12)

That, too, is an expression of a healthy faith. David told God (who
already knew) the precise condition of his heart. And it wasn't pretty. Earlier

in that same psalm, he described this incident from his own life story: "I waited patiently for the LORD; he turned to me and heard my cry. He lifted me out of the slimy pit, out of the mud and mire; he set my feet on a rock and gave me a firm place to stand. He put a new song in my mouth, a hymn of praise to our God" (verses 1-3).

Slimy pits exist in our world just as dark valleys exist. And just as surely as believers must pass through dark valleys, so they occasionally fall into "the mud and mire," needing rescue, cleansing, and comfort.

It's true. It's real. It's the way things are—and David never shrinks from telling it all. Healthy faith helps us embrace who we are, what we are, and where we are. David declares a failing, fallible humanity and a loving, powerful God, who chooses to involve himself in the lives of individual men and women. A healthy faith acknowledges that we are neither infallible nor omniscient nor omnipotent nor omnipresent. (I have met some capable people in my life, but to this day I've never met anyone who could be in two places at the same time!) It's only by dependence on a loving God (who is all those things) that we can get through the shadowed valleys and out of the slimy pits.

Reality says we are the creatures, not the Creator.

We are vulnerable, not invulnerable.

We are flesh and blood, not steel and stone.

We are men and women, not cherubim and seraphim.

We are his sons and daughters; we are not *him*.

We have to embrace the fact that we are a people who must live by grace through faith every day of our lives. I'm impressed that the writer to the Hebrews urged his flock to "encourage one another daily...so that none of you may be hardened by sin's deceitfulness" (Hebrews 3:13). In other words, we need grace, encouragement, wisdom, and mutual accountability *every day of our lives* to keep from being hardened or deceived by sin.

That's the way it is. That's the black and white of it. That is reality. And we must either deny our vulnerability or *deal with it.*

REALITY CAN HURT

Discomfort is reality. Pain is reality. Conflict is reality. Spiritual warfare is reality. Healthy faith helps us embrace all of these biblical realities, *constantly availing ourselves of the reality of Christ's help and presence.* Unhealthy, toxic faith denies the dark side, thus creating an even greater conflict.

A healthy faith accepts who we are and where we are rather than trying to conjure some artificial image for people who are not comfortable accepting us as we are. If we're based in reality, then the reality is that we've *all* failed, we're *all* sinners, and we're *all* stumbling along the way. We thrash about in slimy pits now and then; we feel fear as we walk narrow trails in dark valleys.

In other words, we are 100 percent, certifiably fallible—that is, human. David reminded his readers that God never forgets that fact (even though we may). He wrote: "As a father has compassion on his children, so the LORD has compassion on those who fear him; for he knows how we are formed, he remembers that we are dust" (Psalm 103:13-14).

Some branches of evangelical Christianity teach that believers can achieve a level of "sanctification" where they no longer sin. That is not only unbiblical, it is just plain unrealistic. Reality means seeing, understanding, and accepting the truth about who I am. And how could the old apostle have said it any plainer?

> If we say that we have no sin, we are only fooling ourselves,
> and refusing to accept the truth. But if we confess our sins to
> him, he can be depended on to forgive us and to cleanse us
> from every wrong.... If we claim we have not sinned, we are
> lying and calling God a liar, for he says we have sinned.
> (1 John 1:8-10, TLB)

Do you see what John was saying about living in reality? If we choose the path of deception and deny the obvious truth, in so doing we call God a liar!

If, on the other hand, we walk in reality, that is, "if we walk in the light, as he is in the light, we have fellowship with one another, and the blood of Jesus, his Son, purifies us from all sin" (verse 7). That's where I want to be. Walking in the light. Admitting who I am. Enjoying the companionship of Christian friends and the Lord Jesus himself, experiencing daily cleansing from sin.

Sometimes a believer, while not outwardly denying his own sin, gets so caught up in focusing on the faults and shortcomings of others that he becomes oblivious to his own problems and blind spots. A wife, for instance, may absorb herself in the task of "helping hubby grow and change." Under such pressure, however, that husband may decide he will *never* change or yield ground. But if that wife would begin to face the truth of her own weaknesses, discovering strength and help in the living Christ to gain spiritual ground, she might find she has freed her husband to grow and change in the same way.

THE WAY IT REALLY IS

Growing Christians strive to see the world and their lives as they really are, not through some stained-glass filter, not through the grid of some externally imposed myth or make-believe worldview. They do not feel compelled to "explain away" hardships or events that mystify them, but are willing to live with some ambiguity, trusting God to rule the world in righteousness—even if that means difficulty for them. As with Job, we must sometimes come to that place of humility before God where we say, "Behold, I am insignificant; what can I reply to You? I lay my hand on my mouth" (Job 40:4, NASB).

Healthy faith refuses to sweep suffering, daily struggles with the sinful nature, and inevitable relationship difficulties under a rug, pretending they don't exist. Instead, it brings those issues into the light of Scripture, the scrutiny of the Holy Spirit, and under the mutual counsel and care of trusted brothers and sisters in Christ. Unhealthy faith, on the other hand, denies reality. For those who subscribe to such false belief systems, faith is not based on a belief in the supernatural power of God, but on a desire to see magical solutions that stop pain. They hope in a servant God determined to make life easy.

Healthy faith acknowledges the supernatural power of God and does not need miraculous intervention to prove that God is real. The healthy believer does not look for God to magically change the circumstances, but looks to him in the midst of trials.

Because faith grows strong, there is no need to deny reality. Believing God is faithful to help them through their trials and tribulations, healthy believers have no need to run from reality. They see the problems before them, do what they can to resolve them, and trust God to do the rest. It's dangerous to live any other way. Just ask Rebecca.

REBECCA'S STORY

Rebecca Grant had lived a hard life in the hot desert town of Barstow, California. Her father died when she was very young, and her mother struggled to keep her and her sister in clothes. They rented a small house and her mom worked two jobs. During the day, her mother sold tickets at the Greyhound Bus depot; at night she sold tickets at the theater. On her days off she cleaned the house and did chores. It wasn't a wonderful existence, but her persevering spirit kept the family going.

Rebecca loved her mother and knew how hard she worked to provide the family with the basics of food and clothing. Some of her friends made fun of her because she didn't have a dad and because her mother had to work so much. Their comments bothered Rebecca, but they made her respect her mother even more.

At fourteen, Rebecca began to work. All the money she earned went into a bowl along with her mother's money. They took out only what they needed for the essentials. Rebecca's mother put the rest in a passbook account for the days when Rebecca and her sister would need assistance with college fees.

Rebecca's mother was a woman of faith, a Christian who believed God had a plan for her life. If she was faithful, she believed she would see that plan and God would bless her faithfulness. She didn't waver from her beliefs. In the toughest of times she didn't doubt God's love for her. She trusted him to take care of her and her two daughters. She would do all she could to provide for her family and would leave the rest up to God. She never worked on Sunday and always took the girls to church, where they prayed and sang together.

Rebecca was close to her mother, but not to her mother's God. She enjoyed going to church because of the people there. It was something out of the ordinary routine of the week. She liked it, but she didn't become a Christian. In fact, she doubted there was a God; if he did exist, she felt distant from him. He had never spoken to her or shown himself to her, and he certainly hadn't made life easy for her. She wanted to believe, but she rejected what she heard in church.

What Rebecca heard in her mother's church was a gospel that many preachers dispense, a distortion of truth that is sometimes manipulative. She heard that if a person becomes a Christian, life will become easy. God will take care of everything. Miracles will occur and there will be no more problems. She was told that true believers in Christ are protected from the evil of the world. Faith in Christ was presented as an insurance policy against pain in the present. Rebecca couldn't help but wonder, *If God is so loving, why does he allow my life to be so hard? Why does he force my mother to struggle so much? If there really were a God, he would help us.*

The expectation that faith in God would yield a problem-free life caused Rebecca to abandon her search for truth and latch onto anything that would bring relief. First, she turned to alcohol. Then drugs. Finally, she became so promiscuous that she contracted incurable genital herpes. Her maladies only proved to her that God either did not exist or was not interested in her. Her toxic faith caused her behavior to become increasingly self-destructive.

The Myth of Problem-Free Living

Rebecca's experience is not uncommon. The expectation of an easy life from God has produced more agnostics and atheists than has any other false belief. When people live faithfully but suffer pain and discomfort anyway, many turn from Christianity. They never grasp that a healthy faith does not shield a believer from pain, but rather gives a new perspective on life and a renewed trust in God that lessens the pains of existence. Each time a negative event occurs, God can use it to bring greater faith and deeper peace.

But what many people hear is entirely different. They hear that acceptance of Christ or belief in God causes all problems to vanish; they learn that present problems go away once a person has turned his or her life over to God.

But it just isn't so. That isn't reality.

Those who cling to this unbiblical myth insist: A strong faith will protect me from problems and pain.

How so?

Did it protect James, the brother of John, whom Herod put to death with the sword? Did it protect Jim Elliott from being murdered by Auca Indians in Ecuador? Did it keep Navigators founder Dawson Trotman from drowning in a lake as he attempted to rescue another swimmer? Did it protect Cassie Bernall when she said, "Yes, I believe" to the murderers at Columbine High School?

For many, a belief in God and the practice of faith are just fine until tragedy strikes. Then comes the realization that the practice of faith does not accumulate brownie points of protection. It does not guarantee God's intervention. Bad things do happen to good people, and it has nothing to do with degrees of faith. We live in a world where big animals eat little animals. Decay, rot, and death are realities. Faith provides perspective, perseverance, and purpose through the tough times, but it will not invariably protect anyone from the hard realities of life.

Those who have walked with Christ through the centuries have always been beset by pain, poverty, tragedy, illness, beatings, and other hardships. But the problems helped build their faith, not destroy it. The trials drew believers closer to God because their faith was real *before* the difficulties started.

Those who believe because they want infallible protection have picked the wrong faith; in believing, we often invite problems that we would not have otherwise. So Paul writes, "For it has been granted to you on behalf of Christ not only to believe on him, but also to suffer for him" (Philippians 1:29).

This is one of the problems with faith healing on television. Now, don't get me wrong; I believe God can and does miraculously heal people. But true miracles, by definition, happen rarely. If a healing occurred every time a preacher stood in front of an audience or a television camera, it would not be a miracle, but the norm. Supernatural healing is not the norm. It happens, but usually when the cameras are off.

The problem with claiming "common healing miracles" is that it produces false hope in some and shame in others. Some think that if they can just be good enough, God will heal them. That is not reality. You can't be good enough, because we all mess up every day. If God heals you, it is by his grace, not your goodness. Others think that if they are not healed, then

God is angry with them or their guilt is greater than that of others. This is not reality either. I know personally of instances in which God healed someone in the midst of his or her sin. Their sins were the worst of the worst, but God's grace touched these people, they were healed, and he drew them to Jesus.

The theology of many faith healers has caused serious problems in the Christian church. A great friend of mine is the wife of a man who pastors a charismatic church. They believe in speaking in tongues and in a God who is powerful enough to heal anyone, anywhere, any time. But this dear friend and her husband are rooted and grounded in reality. They believe it is far more important that a heart be healed than an ingrown toenail. They believe God is more concerned about the secrets of the soul than the length of a leg. She said that she and her husband got tired of the show of people falling backward, so they stopped the show and went to work with Jesus on the hearts of their people. They have never been the same, nor has their church.

Be sure that what you look to as evidence of the power of God is real. And do not draw conclusions about God from people who are more focused on a rolling camera than a real God.

THE MYTH OF "INSTANT PEACE"

Another form of denying reality often says words like these: "If I am truly faithful, I will not experience grief, sorrow, anger, or confusion in the face of tragedy or loss. Instead, I will keep my chin up, my eyes dry, my lips smiling, so others will see how strong I am as a Christian. When tragedy strikes, true believers should have real peace about it."

Really? Since when? This serious problem leads to unresolved emotions and a complete split from reality. I have heard people who have lost children, spouses, fortunes, and dreams say that they have this "wonderful peace" just moments after they hear the awful news. What they have is shock, not peace! Shock is a natural reaction designed to protect us, to cushion the reality and depth of our pain and other feelings. Those who profess instant peace will suffer a troubled future full of a greater pain than the original loss and disappointment.

Often those who express their anger and disappointment are challenged to be stronger, to trust more, to find peace. It is true that the genuine believer *will* find peace, but it will be on the other side of resolving the rage that comes with almost every lost expectation. I have heard "spiritual giants" tell people in pain to have more joy. But these sufferers cannot even *spell* joy while trying to grasp a life with the pain of divorce or the void of a lost child. People need time to resolve emotions. Instant peace delays and prolongs the time it takes to adjust and move on to a new life.

Someone will say, "But doesn't Scripture tell us to be thankful in everything?" Yes, it does. But while true faith will lead a person to gratitude for adversity, it is *not* instantaneous. Scripture does not demand that we be grateful instantaneously. It takes time, often lots of time. Those who experience instant peace are not showing instant gratitude to God; they are denying how God made them as physical, spiritual, and emotional beings.

Tragedies bring various responses. God does not seem to deal with them or the people affected by them in a predictable manner. For some, there seems to be a gift of peace that prevents a total collapse. For others, that peace does not surface for months or even years. Whatever the reaction, those who experience peace early are no better or worse, no stronger or weaker. The experience of one person should not be demanded for another. Lack of peace does not mean lack of faith. People in pain do not need sermons on peace. They need love and care and assistance. Remember, faith in God will produce a peace that will go beyond all understanding. It probably won't be an instant peace, but it will be a *real* peace.

THE POLLYANNA MYTH

In this version of warped reality, believers tell themselves, "Everything that happens to me is good."

Who says? Where does the Bible state such a thing?

A godly woman married a man, lived with him ten years, and watched him die of cancer. Another woman in her church insisted she be happy about it: "God has done a good thing. Everything he does is good." Two years later, the woman was married again, and after one year of marriage, her husband died. Again, the lady from church demanded her friend claim this as a great and good victory provided by God. The bereaved woman recovered from her loss, married for a third time, and shortly afterward discovered that her husband had cancer.

This was not good; this was horrible. It comes under the classification of catastrophic loss. There is nothing good about three dead husbands. There is nothing good about a disease that eats your flesh and organs and then leaves you for dead. There is nothing good about watching three men die. To throw this at someone in the midst of such horrible loss is gross insensitivity.

Can God produce something good from it? Oh yes—and he will. That he can take something this horrible and transform it into something powerful for this woman is part of his wonderful and miraculous nature. But first, when we are with someone like her, shouldn't we just be with her? Shouldn't we leave our pat answers at home and just be there and share her grief? I think so. If Jesus can weep at the death of a friend, I think we can weep too. And I think we can weep with others rather than sweep their trauma under the rug of shallow faith.

Some church people believe everything is an immediate blessing. To them, only a real Christian is able to say, "Praise the Lord!" as the house burns down, the car is totaled, a child is hurt, or the cow dies. I believe if you told these people that they were going to be fried in oil, they would grin and say, "Praise the Lord anyway!"

Is this real? Can a person in touch with reality be grateful for times of crisis? Is it a measure of one's faith to be able to greet each new piece of bad news with a big grin and a trite expression? I don't think so. I think it is evidence of unreal people manufacturing an unreal response. They try to rationalize that everything is good, even though it looks bad, feels bad, and is bad. They grow up believing that a positive attitude must be used to face every crisis. They deny how they really feel and thus delay dealing with the pain and agony.

The woman who lost two husbands and was about to lose another was not grateful for their deaths, nor did she believe the events were good. She was quite angry until she resolved her hurt over the losses. Years later she looked back and said that none of the problems was good, but that God used each one for her good. He took the crisis and made it a faith-building experience.

The widow's perspective is much more accurate than the lady who demanded each new loss be viewed as a good thing. They were not good; they were terrible losses. But God takes such losses and over time makes them into something good. God will work everything together for our good if we will allow him to do so. Bad things provide God with a stage to produce something good.

Consider the first time the phrase "not good" is used in Scripture. God himself uses it to describe Adam's condition without a wife. The Lord said, "It is not good for the man to be alone. I will make a helper suitable for him" (Genesis 2:18). Surely if the Lord himself could say it was "not good" for Adam to be alone, we do not have to say it *is* good when a wife or husband is left alone through an untimely death. The Bible does not insist that we call "good" every event that happens in this fallen world. What it does insist is that God will take even the bad events of life and work them together for the good of his children. And that's quite a different thing.

People in pain have enough problems without some well-meaning folks trying to short-circuit the grief process by declaring that everything that happens is a good event sent from God. While God *allows* bad things, he does not *cause* them. The toxic thinking that all things are good makes people wonder whether God might not really be cruel. It forces them to see God as a grim joker who inflicts pain and expects his followers to be happy about it.

This Pollyanna perspective may produce quick relief, but it blocks reality. A loving God wants the best for us and is grieved when we miss it. True faith in him allows these bad things to be woven together in a protective covering that grows stronger in fiber and softer to the touch.

NAIVE FAITH

My mother grew up with a version of warped, unhealthy faith. She believed that dedicating her sons to God would spare them the heartache that other children were forced to endure. She felt that somehow her prayers and faith vaccinated us from evil, that temptations would not likely come our way or, if they did, we would not succumb.

Then her father committed suicide. His death hit her much harder than it would have most people, because she thought she and her family were protected. Still, despite her devastation, she didn't give up her belief in a God who would prevent the natural course of nature or evil from harming her family.

But when my brother contracted AIDS and eventually died, my mother was confronted in a most painful way with the fact that her faith provided no supernatural vaccination against terrible events. She struggled with my brother's illness; she struggled with her faith. She slid into a deep depression, and at times I didn't know if she would return to being the wonderful woman we had always known.

Fortunately, she did recover. How? She dealt with her confusing ideas about faith. She yelled at God. She told him it wasn't fair. She admitted she had come to her faith as a way of making life easier. As she shared her anger and frustration with a God who did not do things according to her fondest wishes and expectations, she slowly recovered from the death of my brother. She also recovered her faith.

Today that faith is whole. It has brought my mother into a new under-standing of who God is and how he works. Today she is more deeply com-mitted and better equipped than ever to help others who are looking for someone who understands.

As I look back on that time, it seems to me that God was building her faith, rooting her more deeply in reality than ever before. When my father died suddenly of a heart attack at the age of sixty-eight, it became apparent that she would need the deeper faith God's grace had forged within her through the death of my brother. My mom and dad loved each other dearly and their lives were each other's. To be left alone so suddenly was a burden she never could have carried with a naive faith. But she did carry that burden, even growing under it. Within a year of Dad's death, Mom was diagnosed with breast cancer. She sailed through what would have wrecked a weaker person. Her ability to accept reality equipped her for a tough turn of events. And through those tough times I watched her grow in wisdom. I am so proud of her and what she has become through the power of God's grace!

YOU'RE NOT ALONE

If you're disillusioned because you were sold a form of faith that didn't pan out, you're not alone. Your pain is shared by many others who must deal with tragedy and at the same time resolve many issues of toxic belief. Their disap-pointments in God increase their pain, just as they may have increased yours.

Let the Great Teacher use your pain to bring you closer to him. It does not have to be a barrier to God. It can be a bridge.

Jesus, the real Son of God who calls us to live in reality, gives us this counsel: "I have told you all this so that you will have peace of heart and mind. Here on earth you will have many trials and sorrows; but cheer up, for I have overcome the world" (John 16:33, TLB).

CHAPTER 2

JUST AS I AM

A Healthy Faith Is Individualized

O LORD, you have searched me and you know me. You know when I sit
and when I rise; you perceive my thoughts from afar. You discern my
going out and my lying down; you are familiar with all my ways.

Psalm 139:1-3

God is big enough to love us individually, call us individually, work with us
individually, and walk with us through life individually, in spite of character
flaws, bad track records, alarming deficiencies, and our own distinctive weaknesses.

In Philippians 3:3, Paul tells the church, in effect, "Listen, we're not
going to hang any of our confidence on human effort. Instead, we're going to
boast about what Christ Jesus has done for each one of us, in particular,
whatever our backgrounds or gifts. God loves each one of us as individuals."
Many times we feel we can't live up to what God wants for us, that we don't
have what it takes, that we're not good enough, that we're not doing enough.
It's important to remember Paul's words: "It's not the human effort or background that counts; it is Jesus Christ."

If you look at verse 5 in that same chapter, you see Paul talking about
himself as one of the Pharisees, those who demanded strictest obedience to

the Jewish law. These were the people Jesus struggled against so often. They focused on human effort and not on the transforming power of God, and so they failed to please the Lord.

God doesn't want us continually comparing ourselves with others, saying to ourselves, "Well, there are the really spiritual folks, there are those who are next to the best, and then there's me—a charter member of the 'barely adequate' group." He knows your weaknesses very well (who better?), accepts those weaknesses, and loves you in spite of them.

His individualized love does not mean that he approves of everything you do or applauds all that you lack. Each one of us has our own set of struggles in the Christian life. Some might boast that they've never been tempted to drink, do drugs, or chase someone else's mate. But is that something to boast about? Maybe the way you were raised spared you from those problems. You might have more trouble with pride or gossip or secret idolatries. God doesn't approve of those things either. But he loves you, and for as long as you live he's going to work with you on those areas.

We need to let his loyal love move and motivate us to bring our lives into alignment with his. As we obey, saying "yes" to his Spirit in an increasing way, we grow in holiness.

INDIVIDUALIZED NEEDS

I know of a couple who were planning a party on a large boat for their son's twenty-first birthday. After they made the reservation, but before the party, they discovered their son was involved in a homosexual relationship. Crushed and angry, the father immediately declared, "We are *not* going through with this party. We're going to kick this boy out of our home. We're going to have nothing to do with him or any of his friends."

When I heard about this man's response, I felt a sense of alarm. I knew that if these parents followed through with this course of action, they would lose their son forever. They would be cutting off any potential relationship with him. They would be saying that they had no desire or intention to help him with some deep, troubling needs. Yes, he was choosing to meet those needs in an immoral way. But this mom and dad might be his only link to Jesus Christ. If they ever wanted him to abandon his sinful lifestyle, they would have to stick with him.

Fortunately, they got some good counsel: "Don't cancel the party, or essentially you're canceling the relationship." So they went ahead with their original plans. It was difficult for them and their hearts ached for what had been lost. But they kept their heads high and celebrated the day with their boy. And now, if their son ever has any desire to turn his life around and practice the faith of his childhood, that door is wide open. He knows his mother and father condemn his lifestyle; they have made their feelings and beliefs quite clear. But they've also made themselves available, just as Jesus made himself available to men and women who were shunned and despised by the masses.

I know this approach is hard for many Christians. They believe it is their job to inflict shame on a grown man, rather than show him there is always an open door. As a result, we have lost many hurting sons and daughters to those who *are* willing to be with them. We should not condone sinful behavior any more than Jesus approved of the activities of the woman at the well or the woman caught in adultery. But Jesus focused more on *connection* than *correction*. He knew that when the connection grew strong, so would the desire to do the correct thing. As parents, we should use these two biblical incidents as models. We are not called to enable our children's sin, but neither are we called to enrage our children against us. We must show them love, especially when it is difficult to do so.

Remember Zacchaeus, the little tax collector who had betrayed his nation and cheated his fellow countrymen out of their wages? When Jesus announced the salvation of that despised man, he knew Zacchaeus was every bit as repugnant to the people of his day as those living a homosexual lifestyle might be to us today. Yet Jesus stood with that man in front of the crowd, probably with an arm draped over his shoulder, and said, "Today salvation has come to this house, because this man, too, is a son of Abraham. For the Son of Man came to seek and to save what was lost" (Luke 19:9-10). But before Jesus could announce the salvation of this wee little man, he had to go to his house. He had to associate with him, connect with him, even when it made Jesus look bad to those who did not understand what good really was.

Jesus was available to those who needed him so desperately. We need to adopt that same attitude. Available. Open. Compassionate. Ready to talk. Ready to teach. Ready to help. If you see someone caught in some sin, don't just cover him with a convenient, blanket label as "sinner." No. Look at that person's individual needs. What has he been through? How can you model Jesus to him? And remember, at the same time, Jesus is dealing with *your* unique needs, weaknesses, and character defects.

Many people steeped in religion would rather be "right" than in relationship with anyone they think is in the wrong. But God has not called us to "rightness." He has called us into relationship with himself and with other men and women. As John wrote, "If anyone says, 'I love God,' yet hates his brother, he is a liar. For anyone who does not love his brother, whom he has seen, cannot love God, whom he has not seen. And he has given us this command: Whoever loves God must also love his brother" (1 John 4:20-21). And what of those who are in the wrong? Hear Paul's counsel: "The Lord's servant must not quarrel; instead, he must be kind to everyone, able to teach, not resentful. Those who oppose him he must gently instruct, in the hope that God will grant them repentance leading them to a knowledge of the truth, and that they will come to their senses and escape from the trap of the devil, who has taken them captive to do his will" (2 Timothy 2:24-26).

It all stems from walking *as an individual* with the Lord Jesus Christ. As John wrote, "We proclaim to you what we have seen and heard, so that you also may have fellowship with us. And our fellowship is with the Father and with his Son, Jesus Christ" (1 John 1:3).

Did you ever think about that? One of your primary callings as a believer is to be in fellowship with God and his Son. To walk with him, talk with him, know his mind, and sense the yearnings of his heart. In God's way of looking at things, that counts for a lot more than conforming to some image or standard set forth by others. It is your individual walk with Jesus Christ that is of primary importance! There was a time when I forgot that.

REGAINING A SENSE OF INDIVIDUALITY

I've always been a person who appreciated humor—perhaps to a fault. I love to joke and I'm always looking for the humor in every situation. No matter where I'm ministering, I like to find something funny in a given set of circumstances and talk about that. I want people to enjoy themselves.

In my college days, I used to love cracking people up by throwing in comments to lighten up otherwise tense or tedious situations. When I came back to the faith, I was under the impression that I had to give up humor (or at least cut it back to the nub) and become very solemn and serious. Soon the part of me that loved to smile and laugh began to wither.

And yet I didn't want it to wither! I didn't want that aspect of my personality to die. It was a unique part of me that God had created. In reality, it was one of my best strengths. Over time, I began to see the futility of trying to change my identity to fit someone else's mold of what Steve Arterburn should be and do. For one thing, I really didn't like that "mold." (It felt "moldy" and unattractive.) So, over time, once more I began to use humor in my life and ministry. Or rather I began to let the humor come out again—it had been hiding in a corner of my soul all along! Now, I am rediscovering what a strength that aspect of my personality can be in communicating truth and grace to others.

What did it take to get me to change? I finally had to admit that I could no longer fake it. And then I had to ask God to give me wisdom and discernment and strength to develop this aspect of my life that I had shelved for so long. In God's timing, the humor and love of fun came back better than ever. I didn't need to rely on crude or off-color stuff; I could simply let the life of Christ shine through me in the way he intended. It was fun to be me again!

I don't believe God ever intended us to stifle our personality in order to conform to some starchy image of what we imagine a "good Christian" should look and sound like. Pastor Chuck Swindoll used to tell of the early days of his ministry in New England, when he tried to walk, talk, and preach like one of his most admired mentors. It didn't work. His ministry (if you can imagine such a thing happening to Swindoll) went nowhere. It was only as he began to be himself—relaxed, cutting up at times, laughing out loud in the pulpit if he felt like it—that God began to use his preaching in a powerful way.

God wanted Chuck to be Chuck. And he wants you to be you.

Picture a bright, creative, artistic woman who comes to Jesus Christ. Before her conversion, she is active in the community, exercises leadership, and is outgoing and vivacious in all her social contacts. Then she becomes a believer, and within her particular fellowship, she is given the impression that to fit the mold of a Christian woman she must become a doormat at home, wear dresses that cover the ankle, and become a meek and colorless maidservant. What happens to this woman? Something in her begins to die, and the strain of "playing a part" begins to wear away at her personality, until she finally says to herself, "This isn't working. How can I better use and develop my strengths and my personality, rather than kill them for Christ? How can I bring them under control and develop them in an appropriate way? How can I be a more attractive Christian, rather than a constrained and boring person who's overly serious for the sake of creating some image to please others?"

Sadly, Christians who come to this point are often criticized or even persecuted for insisting that they be who God made them to be. People who use others for power, profit, prestige, and pleasure are not going to go along with such freedom! When I counsel with those who are struggling in such settings, I prepare them for the rejection and hostility they are bound to experience. If they disagree with the pastor, they're going to be called a sower of discord. If they disagree openly, they'll be accused of having a spirit of rebellion.

Fortunately, God is strong enough to get people through the criticism or persecution should they break the mold and begin "being themselves" again for Jesus' sake. People with a healthy faith depend upon God for their strength. That strength will get them through the inevitable reaction, pressure, and criticism of those who run with the pack and can't accept an individualized walk with God. Healthy faith allows us to express faith as individuals, not just as conformists to some rigid religious system.

When my [Jack's] children were small, I attended Newport Christian Center. The pastor at that time, Jim Bradford, knew of some of my abilities and talents and wanted me to step into a teaching and administrative counseling position at the church. Determining to be candid with this good shepherd, I told him, "You know, right now, at this time of my life, with all I've got on my plate...I just want to relax."

I braced myself for all the guilt and shame you might expect a pastor to heap on you when he wants something. But Pastor Bradford surprised me.

"Well," he said, "if you're not there to do it, Jack, and even if it doesn't get done, then it wasn't what God wanted. No big deal. We're behind you. We're here for *you*, you're not here for us."

Oh man! You can't believe how freeing those comments were to me. He was saying, "Jack, you're free to give to the church and free to minister when you're ready. You're also free to say no to a request for service and free to disagree with the leadership. You're free to come and you're free to go. There's no condemnation. The church is truly here for you. It's God's church, not the pastor's church or the elders' church. Until God moves you to minister in some capacity, relax and soak up the teaching and fellowship. Worship God with us."

THE DANGER OF COOKIE-CUTTER CHRISTIANITY

Healthy, growing Christians know that they are unique creations of an infinitely creative God. They have their own distinctive, personal identity and do not strive to mirror the personality or unique gifts of another. They are not cookie-cutter Christians and do not attempt to shove others into their own mold.

Sometimes people do not want to be Christians because either they know they are nothing like the people who claim to be Christians or they don't want to be like the ones they see. Many Christians are trying to act as they think they are "supposed to act" rather than how they really are. They do not believe God values their unique personality. So rather than being the person they are, they try to become like the pack—even if it means losing their creativity and strength. The truth is, if they would just dedicate their uniqueness to God, he would do great things with it. And their faith would grow vital and strong. They would feel God's unconditional love rather than feel as if they really did not fit in God's family.

J. B. Phillips's paraphrase of Romans 12:2 says, "Don't let the world around you squeeze you into its own mould, but let God re-make you so that your whole attitude of mind is changed. Thus you will prove in practice that the will of God is good, acceptable to him and perfect."

Isn't that good? Let God do the molding in your life! Let him do the shaping and crafting and refining, and let him do it from the inside out. Don't let others, no matter how sincere and helpful they may be, mold you from the outside in! After all, how do *they* know what sort of person (or personality) God wants within his family in a given place to accomplish his purposes?

How sad it is to realize that many people never come to Christ because they do not understand that God's love is individualized. They never come to that sweet, liberating understanding that God calls them to faith as individuals—that he wants them just as they are.

Let me give you the good news. God's family is big enough for you.

God's love is wide enough, deep enough, and complete enough for you, even if you don't look a bit like your preconceived notion of what a real Christian ought to look like. You can come as you are as an individual, and God will accept you as an individual and work with you as an individual. You may trust him and live your life according to how the Holy Spirit leads you, and God will guide your way. God loves us as individuals; it was he who created our uniquenesses. Each of us has a unique place and a unique purpose in his family and in his church.

Ephesians 4:11 tells us that some of us have been given preaching gifts. Others are better at serving and caring for members of the church. God has made us uniquely for service to one another. When we abandon that uniqueness, we abandon God's will for our lives.

A healthy church is made up of individuals with a full range of emotions, intellect, free will, and the ability to function independently. God has created each person individually in his own image. He does not want to waste the uniqueness of any of us. He has given us many unique gifts that he wants us to develop in service to him. The church is one body of many members. We must continue to come together as a group so that God can use our individual gifts for the benefit of all who worship him. As healthy faith grows, shame diminishes, and we delight in finding that we do not have to live in the image of another person—only in the image of God.

FIG PICKERS ANONYMOUS

When I think of unique individuals, my mind settles on Amos, a most unrefined prophet of the Lord. Amos was no Isaiah, no D. James Kennedy in a blue suit. Those who know the intricacies of ancient Hebrew say that his use of language is simple and crude compared to the more complex, courtly language of Isaiah. And some of those in the religious hierarchy of Amos's day did not appreciate his ordinary exterior.

The high priest of the northern kingdom, in fact, became disgusted and enraged by Amos's prophecies of doom for rebellious Israel. He sneered at the rawboned, rough-hewn prophet from the south. "Amaziah said to Amos, 'Get out, you seer! Go back to the land of Judah. Earn your bread there and do your prophesying there. Don't prophesy anymore at Bethel, because this is the king's sanctuary and the temple of the kingdom'" (Amos 7:12-13).

The prophet's answer is classic. He refused to be intimidated by the arrogant priest. Instead of trying to fit into some classic prophet mold, Amos simply spoke the blunt truth. He told Amaziah, "I was neither a prophet nor a prophet's son, but I was a shepherd, and I also took care of sycamore-fig trees. But the LORD took me from tending the flock and said to me, 'Go, prophesy to my people Israel.' Now then, hear the word of the LORD" (verses 14-16).

Isn't that great? "Hey, Amaziah, I never asked to be a prophet. I'm just a shepherd and a fig picker. But God gave me a job to do, so I'm going to do it. Now listen up!"

If God had wanted a polished Isaiah or a prophet of royal blood like Zephaniah, he could have called someone like that. But he didn't. God had a particular voice, a particular style, and a particular physical presence in mind. So he found Amos up on his stepladder picking figs, tapped him on the shoulder, and said, "Come on down, son. I have a job for you."

ARE YOU A VOLVO OR A MUSTANG?

The Bible presents an amazing collection of characters—real characters!—whom God chose to use and bless in incredible, powerful ways. It's as though he toured used-car lots and junkyards, picking a strange collection of old pickups, orange Volkswagens, Ford Pintos, outsized '70s vintage Pontiacs and Mercurys, and reconditioned Humvees to develop into a fleet of kingdom racecars. He doesn't want a convoy of identical white Dodge Caravans all rolling along at the same speed. This is a Creator who delights in individuality and variety. (If you don't believe it, visit an ocean aquarium or leaf through your old high-school yearbook. Strange creatures abound!)

Think back to the group of twelve he chose to be with him and represent him while he walked this earth: crusty fishermen, a reconstructed radical, a despised Roman collaborator, a man who struggled with doubt. Then, to round out the picture, he added Saul of Tarsus—the church's most bitter and bloody enemy.

Since God first walked with Adam in the garden, he has chosen the most unbelievable collection of common laborers, priests and prostitutes, queens and statesmen, fugitives and artisans, celebrities and men and women off the street to carry his message and represent his name to a cynical, often hostile world.

And he has a role for each one of us, too, just as we are. He knows how to smooth out the rough edges. He knows how to surgically remove sinful aspects from a unique personality. He knows how to teach us and lead us to become the men and women he intended us to be before the foundation of the world. We need to get out of his way—and out of each other's way—to let that process go forward.

Paul speaks bluntly to this issue in 2 Corinthians 10. With his ironic, sarcastic tone firmly in place, he writes: "We do not dare to classify or compare ourselves with some who commend themselves." And then he adds this bit of wisdom: "When they measure themselves by themselves and compare themselves with themselves, they are not wise" (verse 12).

It is *never* wise to let comparisons leave us discouraged. My background is not your background. My gifts are not your gifts. My experience with Jesus Christ is not your experience with Jesus Christ. My personality package is not your personality package. My sins and struggle areas are probably not your sins and struggle areas. We are different! God calls us as individuals into his great, diverse family that stretches across time and around the world.

Remember, it is God himself who delights to blend such a wild collection of individuals, gifts, strengths, and weaknesses into a living, ministering body that brings great glory to his Son...and endless delight to the heart of the Father.

CHAPTER 3

GROUND ZERO

A Healthy Faith Is Focused on the True God

"Love the Lord your God with all your heart and with all your soul and
with all your mind." This is the first and greatest commandment.
Matthew 22:37-38

It has never been easier or more convenient for a believer to lose focus on the
one true God. If the apostle Paul found himself "greatly distressed" to note
that Athens was "full of idols" (Acts 17:16), he'd be even more upset after
checking out today's Internet.

A recent *Wall Street Journal* article quotes an Internet guru who plugged
the word "God" into a popular search engine. He received 600,000 responses—remarkably close to the 775,000 sites listed for "sex." Yahoo, Inc.,
lists 17,000 sites devoted to religion and spirituality, compared with 12,000
about movies and 600 about home and garden. And the number of religious
sites is expanding *exponentially*. Seekers are a mouse click away from countless links, Web pages, and chat rooms, each willing to define God, redefine
him, make him over into their own image, or explain him out of existence
altogether.

You could almost believe the apostle had today in mind when he wrote
to his young friend, "Timothy, guard what has been entrusted to your care.

Turn away from godless chatter and the opposing ideas of what is falsely called knowledge, which some have professed and in so doing have wandered from the faith" (1 Timothy 6:20-21).

With all of this information and all these options at our fingertips, it is more important than ever that we stay focused on the true God and his Son, Jesus, not allowing ourselves to be sidetracked into areas of false teaching that could prove destructive to our faith.

When you stop to think about it, the key to just about everything lies in *focus.*

The writer to the Hebrews called it "fixing our thoughts" and "fixing our eyes." "Therefore, holy brothers, who share in the heavenly calling, *fix your thoughts on Jesus,* the apostle and high priest whom we confess.... Let us *fix our eyes on Jesus,* the author and perfecter of our faith" (Hebrews 3:1; 12:2). In other words, rivet your attention on Jesus. Lock onto God's Son for dear life. Even when distractions around you seem overpowering. Even when your heart is breaking.

THE JESUS GAUGE

A psychologist friend recently told me about a client he described as "a believer after God's own heart." Cliff had a singular motivation to please God and serve him. He worked at his job to serve the Lord first and earn a living second. He dedicated himself to the needs of others and genuinely enjoyed meeting those needs. "Healthy" is almost too feeble a word to describe such a robust faith.

After many years of service to Christ, Cliff's wife developed a quickly spreading cancer. Although many people joined Cliff in fervent prayer for his wife, she failed rapidly and soon died. Through it all, however, Cliff did not break his determined gaze on Christ. Instead of allowing the tragedy to shake his faith, he allowed his deep experience of pain and suffering—and even depression and confusion—to push him even deeper into the arms of the living God.

This grieving servant of God knew only two things to hold on to, and he held on to both with all his might. The first was his unshakable conviction that God was a good God. And while he didn't understand this particular circumstance or why his wife had to suffer and die, he did know that God was good and that there had to be a reason he would come to understand one day. And second, he knew beyond all doubt that God loved him. In spite of everything. No matter what. Through it all.

Cliff clung to those twin truths, refusing to take his eyes off the Lord even when he was wracked with grief.

When you're in severe pain or distress, life becomes pretty simple. You're in survival mode, and you have neither the heart nor the strength to spread around your emotional energy. As Chuck Swindoll might say, "Life gets boiled down to the nubbies." Instrument-certified pilots know what this is all about. When visibility drops to nil and storms rage around them, it is second nature for them to focus on the "artificial horizon" gauge on their instrument panel. No matter what their senses might tell them or what weird phenomena they see through the windscreen, they know that gauge will give them their true position and keep them flying level. They may feel as though they are in a steep dive—or even flying upside down. Yet their eyes must lock onto that gauge, and they must respond accordingly. When it comes to survival, it doesn't really matter what they *feel* like; what matters is what their instruments say.

As I write these words, the nation is grieving over the loss of John F. Kennedy, Jr., his wife, Carolyn, and her sister. I never met this handsome young man, but I grew up with him. I never shook his hand, but I will always remember his hand held in salute as his father's coffin passed by him. Grief and sadness have emerged from my anger. Anger? Yes—anger that he took himself and two wonderful women from the top of the sky to the bottom of the ocean. Anger that he did not know how to use the instruments that could have saved their lives. Reports say he was flying at night, in a haze, and over water. Any one of these three conditions requires flying by instruments. His lack of knowledge forced him to rely on how he felt, and his feelings flew him fast toward a watery grave. His gaze and focus were off. He needed a guide outside himself. Without it, his disorientation led to tragedy.

Many travel through this world basing every decision they make on how they feel and what they experience. They do not study God's Word or spend time with Jesus; they have no real knowledge of this Guide who begs us to follow him, no matter how we feel and regardless of our circumstances. If we stay focused on him, if it becomes second nature to look to him and not to ourselves, we will not get lost in the dark. Jesus will be that instrument that keeps us headed toward the horizon. Our faith in him can keep us from altering our direction based on momentary discomfort—and it can prevent needless tragedy.

So it was with Cliff. Although his emotions sometimes raged and other times fell dead flat, although his thoughts were at times confused and he felt his equilibrium slipping, he focused on the "Jesus gauge." He knew that no matter how his circumstances changed, his Lord would neither change nor fail. As the Lord told Israel, "I the LORD do not change. So you, O descendants of Jacob, are not destroyed" (Malachi 3:6). As a consequence of such focus, Cliff enjoyed a daily supply—an artesian well—of God's love through those days of sorrow and distress. He was not only comforted himself, but he became a surprising source of comfort to others.

Our faith, when focused on the true God, will not be shaken by adversity or unexpected turbulence. As long as we, like Cliff, hold tight to our faith in God's goodness and love, we can come through pain and struggle with a deeper and richer relationship with Jesus, rather than a faith strained beyond its limits because we failed to focus on the true God.

MORE JESUS, LESS RELIGION?

Some who notice the title of this book—*More Jesus, Less Religion*—might take offense at our focus on "more Jesus." They might say, "How can this book be about healthy faith if you're saying there's only one way to God? After all, doesn't spirituality in America these days embrace all faiths?" They would be disturbed that two guys like us would narrowly define "healthy faith" with the claim that Jesus is the only way to the true and living God.

A few years ago, a friend of ours wrote a children's book about heaven. On a whim, he decided to check out the reviews of his book on a major bookseller's Web site. One reviewer said that she had been attracted by the title of the book and enchanted by the rich artwork. She noted that she had been looking forward to reading the book to her children. But imagine her dismay when she discovered that the author claimed Jesus was the only way to heaven. Deeply offended by the book's "obvious bias against non-Christians," she deemed it "inappropriate for children." After thinking about it for a while, our author friend decided it was an excellent review.

These are the days of tolerance and diversity in all things—and religion in particular. Hinduism is a diverse and tolerant religion, embracing many of the priorities and positive character qualities we endorse in Christianity. In fact, Hindus view Jesus as one of the many manifestations of God, an incarnation of the impersonal "Brahman." According to that religion, Jesus is merely one of many ways for a person to find God and eternal life. I respect the dedication and devotion to their faith that I see in so many Hindus. Many are more truly dedicated to the spiritual things of life than some Christians I know. They are quite sincere in their search for God.

But I've noticed something about Hindu literature, something that moves me to unspeakable gratitude that I believe as I do about Jesus. Hindu writings are full of words such as "attain," "endeavor," "strive," and "achieve." When you read these words (and so many others like them) in various religious systems, and when you talk to their adherents about a relationship with God and finding eternal life, you hear things like, "Well, we just have to be good people. We have to do good things, and if we live a good life, we just might make it."

It amazes me to hear how often people caught in a crime or some compromising position say, "Sure, I made a mistake. But you really shouldn't judge me by this one incident. Basically, I'm a good person." How grateful I am that I do not believe the criteria for entering heaven is being a "good person" or having a sufficient list of "good accomplishments"! Because, in all candor, *I am not a "basically good person," nor do I have nearly enough brownie points on my scorecard to get me six inches off the ground toward heaven.* If the criteria for eternal life were goodness and good deeds, I would be in last place. In fact, I would have a confirmed reservation in the west wing of hell. So I praise my God and Savior every day that "human goodness" is not one of the criteria he uses to allow people into his heaven!

Just last week my wife and I had lunch with a non-Christian friend. As we ate, we began to discuss spiritual things, and when I referred to the parable of the prodigal son, no recognition lit up his face. He had never heard the story; he knew almost nothing about the Bible.

As we talked he got around to stating his theology: namely, good people make it to heaven. He viewed himself as a kind, loving, and good person. Indeed, he has to be one of the nicest people I have ever met. But as we talked longer, he discussed his Internet relationships with women who were ready to leave their husbands to live with him. His "goodness," as he called it, had given them a new hope to survive.

I felt compelled to challenge his thinking and theology. "What would these *husbands* think of your 'goodness'?" I asked him. "Out of 'goodness,' have you ever called one of these men and asked if he minded your having an Internet relationship with his wife?" Of course, he had not. Suddenly he understood that what might be good for one person can be very bad for someone else.

I am so grateful that I do not have to go through this world trying to figure out if my deeds "measure up," if they are good for me and everyone else. I have always failed at such a system—and will continue to fail for the rest of my life.

A Basic Question

But that still leaves us with a problem. How can a loving God allow only those who believe a certain way to enter heaven? How can faith be healthy and full of love if it begins with the premise that some very generous and loving people will be excluded from eternal life in the presence of God?

These are good questions, and they prompt another basic question: If God really is God, isn't he entitled to have certain criteria to determine who can have a relationship with him and one day enter his home? After all, you probably have criteria for people entering *your* home; you don't allow just anybody to waltz in through the front door and check out your refrigerator whenever they please. As an individual, you also have criteria regarding those with whom you form relationships. You don't enter into a loving, close, personal relationship with someone at random—say, pick a name out of the Cincinnati phone book. So if *you* have criteria, doesn't *God* have the right to set up some criteria?

I look at that question and say, "Well, of course! He's God. He can have anything he wants." It just makes sense that God would have criteria. And if his criteria include you and me having to live up to a certain standard—whether it's the Ten Commandments or the Two Commandments—I know that I cannot consistently live up to those standards. I am not good enough. I will *never* be good enough.

So I'm thrilled that along the way my parents introduced me to what God chose as his single criterion: his Son. God said, "Look at all those people down there. They can *never* meet my standards of goodness." When Adam choked, we all became helpless members of the "Adam's Family!" We are messed up beyond belief, and God understands that better than anyone. So the criterion for a relationship with him couldn't be goodness or good works—otherwise no one would have a relationship with God. Not Florence Nightingale. Not D. L. Moody. Not Billy Graham. No one! As the psalmist wrote, "If you, O LORD, kept a record of sins, O Lord, who could stand? But with you there is forgiveness; therefore you are feared" (Psalm 130:3-4).

Nevertheless, there have to be criteria for a relationship between God and man, for God is not only loving, but holy. And to come into his presence, we must be holy too. So God sent Jesus to die on the cross to take care of all of our unholiness. All we have to do is accept Jesus. That is God's sole criterion for our being in relationship with him. We accept Jesus' death and resurrection as the truths that offset our utter inability to be good enough or do enough good things to enter into heaven. And so when we focus on the true God, we must focus on Jesus.

In Matthew 11:27, Jesus said: "All things have been handed over to Me by My Father; and no one knows the Son except the Father; nor does anyone know the Father except the Son, and anyone to whom the Son wills to reveal Him" (NASB). Jesus meant that he and God are one, and the only way for a person to come into relationship with God is through Jesus. The apostles understood this to be his meaning, for in Acts 4:12, Peter says of Jesus Christ, "Salvation is found in no one else, for there is no other name under heaven given to men by which we must be saved."

This truth eliminates the possibility that Jesus might be some vague manifestation of an impersonal God. It eliminates the possibility that he could be classified merely as a "good and wise man" who walked the face of the earth and loved people. It shows that Jesus is either the true God, on whom we must focus, or he was a colossal fraud, and the countless thousands who have suffered and died for him down through the millennia made a horrible and tragic mistake.

John 5:24 says, "Truly, truly, I say to you, he who hears My word, and believes Him who sent Me, has eternal life, and does not come into judgment, but has passed out of death into life" (NASB). Focusing our belief on Jesus prevents us from having to be judged on our own goodness; instead we can be judged by Christ's goodness and his ability to take care of the sin in our lives.

John 5:23 tells us that "he who does not honor the Son does not honor the Father who sent him." So if you want a relationship with the true God, you must have a relationship with Jesus, his Son. It's not just the best option; it is the only option.

Many of us have been fascinated by stories of out-of-body experiences by people who claim to have died and been resuscitated or who have come close to death. Some of these folks claim they have been to heaven and have seen what is there. While details of their observations differ greatly from one another, most report one common phenomenon: a source of light.

These out-of-body experiences are not new. In fact, the first one I ever read about occurred in the first century. The apostle Paul writes about it in a letter to the church in Corinth. He tells of God taking him up into heaven and admits, "Whether it was in the body or out of the body I do not know" (2 Corinthians 12:2). He saw things there he was not allowed to describe. But one grand and glowing reality emerges from his experience, a truth that convinced him there was only one criterion for entering heaven: God's Son.

When Paul came back he did not forsake his deep beliefs in Jesus because heaven was full of worshipers of Buddha or Mohammed. No! In fact, he was jailed, beaten, starved, tortured, and eventually killed because he would not stop talking about Jesus as the only Savior of the world. He did not change his tune after seeing heaven, but instead sang that tune louder and louder until he took his last breath. I have to believe that if there were "some other way," Paul would never have endured what he did.

More Walk, Less Talk

I'm also convinced that people who are focused on the true God *talk* a lot less about God and *do* a lot more for him and in his name. I was captivated by a story in a recent issue of the *Orange County Register,* profiling top high-school graduates in Orange County, California.

The headline read: "Seniors and their inspirational mentors." At the top of the page was a picture of a mother and daughter, two attractive women who could easily pass for sisters. Tiffany Potter, the daughter, a senior at Liberty Christian High School, wrote the accompanying story. She said that her mother inspired her desire to excel and described how her mother had taken an active interest in her academic life from earliest memory. She credited her mom with instilling good work habits and ethics in her heart. According to Tiffany, her mom had always been her greatest model and by far was the strongest woman she had ever known. Tiffany's mother modeled the true God, and this daughter saw that modeling not only through the good and golden times, but even more through the difficult and trying times.

Although she was a single, working woman, this godly mother managed to pay her daughter's way through a private high school on a very small Christian school teacher's salary, which she supplemented with money from tutoring students after hours. Yet Tiffany says she never remembers "going without." Somehow, all of her needs (and even many of her desires) were met along the way.

It was from her mother that Tiffany learned what it meant to face adversity. In December of Tiffany's senior year, after raising enough money to send her daughter to Florida for Christmas, this hard-working mom was diagnosed with breast cancer. She underwent chemotherapy every two weeks for nine months and radiation every day for six weeks after that. Yet she continued to work full time and tutor on the side. After being diagnosed with breast cancer, she had purchased a home, almost paid off her car, and underwritten Tiffany's excellent education at Liberty Christian.

Tiffany closed her article with these words: "She has always told me that one person with courage makes a majority. And, do not go where the road may take you; instead, go where there is no road, and make a path. She also taught me to have faith in the Lord and trust in him. My prayer is that one day I may become even half the mother that my mother is."[1]

Tiffany is a blessed young woman to have a model so focused on the true, living God. Tiffany's mother emphasized the important issues of life with her daughter, successfully laying foundational blocks of a healthy faith. Too many parents focus on relatively minor issues, nitpicking over small things, trying to eliminate quirks in a child's life that might make them look like bad parents. Tiffany reminds me of the necessity of "majoring on the majors" in parenting: connecting with that child, laying the foundation stones, and modeling God through sacrifice and determination, whatever life's adversities.

SINGLE FOCUS, EXPANDED VISION

If there's anything I've learned since writing *Toxic Faith,* it's that the true God of the universe is far more loving and full of grace than I ever imagined. Yes, God is holy and we need to focus on his holiness and do whatever it takes to become more like him, surrendering ourselves so that the Holy Spirit can do this transforming work. But we also need to step back and realize how *big* a God we really serve. Over the years, my view of the Lord has been growing. At the same time, I've become increasingly aware that not everyone in God's family looks, talks, or thinks like me. Not everyone is on the same spiritual page as I am. Many are much further along in their spiritual growth; they enjoy a dimension to their faith and an intimacy with Christ that I can only dream about. I'm simply not there yet. Others are barely out of spiritual diapers, knowing very little of God's attributes and ways.

But you know what?

God is big enough to receive all who accept his Son, Jesus. At the same time, he is in the process of wooing and drawing all types of men, women, and children to himself. He is using every person and circumstance imaginable to draw people into his loving embrace. For some it's success that provides the crucial nudge. For others, it is some appalling failure or incredible life crisis. But through it all, he loves us and relentlessly calls us to the cross…the ultimate, blood-soaked meeting ground for God and man.

THE FOCUS OF YOUR LIFE

When Jesus walked this earth, he worked to get the focus off "good" people doing what appeared to be "good things" and to get their focus back on God. Many people in first-century Israel were pointing to the rules; Jesus pointed to a God who wanted a relationship with his people. Religious professionals focused on the law; Jesus focused on the Lawgiver who knew our hearts and offered us grace in the midst of our failures.

A healthy, growing faith is always focused on the person of God himself, not on cheap substitutes. A healthy faith begins and ends in God, not in rules or regulations or sheer, raw duty. Jesus, not religion, is at the core of a robust Christian faith.

Today Jesus offers you and me the same opportunity he gave to those people in the early church. Oh, we can still perform and conform out of obligation. We can still try to feel good by all the "good deeds" we chalk up.

Or we can love God with all our heart, mind, and soul. We can experience his love and come to know him intimately. We can stop hiding behind our facades of religious order and meet him right where we are. We can focus on him and find sanity, rest, and peace when all hell seems to be breaking out around us.

I urge you to experience for yourself his love and acceptance. Grow closer to him and choose him because you truly love him. Make *him*—not your "good deeds" nor anyone or anything else—the focus of your life.

I promise...you will never regret it.

CHAPTER 4

HANDING OVER THE KEYS

A Healthy Faith Is Trusting

In God I trust; I will not be afraid. What can mortal man do to me?

Psalm 56:4

There is one huge reason why people don't trust God more fully.

It's not that they don't want to.

It's not that they're incapable of it.

It's not that they trust only themselves.

It's because they don't believe God truly loves them.

Most people can accept that God, to be God, has to be almighty. It's no great stretch to believe that the Creator of the universe sees everything, knows everything, and can do anything. For many, trust doesn't question God's *ability* to meet our needs, but rather his *willingness* and *desire*. We think, *Sure, he could take care of me...but why should he? Why should he love me, forgive me, bear with me, stand by me, and respond to me?*

STEVE'S TESTIMONY

It wasn't too long ago that such thinking was exactly my problem. I had trouble trusting the Lord. I would tell myself I was "surrendered to God," but then I would turn around and grab things back from him. In so many areas of life I felt like I had to push, manipulate, cajole, and use all my wiles and persuasive abilities to make things happen—even things that God may not have wanted to happen.

Because my belief in God's love was weak, my ability to trust him was weak. I was afraid to let him in on my business deals or financial arrangements or future plans. I can see now how different life could have been if I had only trusted him. If I had just said, "Lord, what do *you* want? Is this something that would please you?", then maybe I wouldn't have made so many mistakes in business and ministry and relationships.

I remember a story I heard about a missionary in some remote village in the Andes. One day he was driving along in his little pickup and saw an old woman bent over under the weight of the large, heavy basket she carried on her back. He offered her a ride in the back of his pickup and she shyly accepted. As he drove along, however, he noticed the woman squatting in the back of the truck with that basket still on her back. He stopped the truck for a moment and tried to explain that she no longer had to carry that heavy cargo; the truck would easily bear them both to their destination. Yet she couldn't seem to understand. She imagined that she had to carry the weight even as the truck was carrying her.

Once I began to understand that God could carry both me and all my responsibilities and problems, I began to relax. And I found myself better able to connect with others, loving them in a deeper way. Before, I had used all my energy on the burdens. I tried to keep all of them balanced on my back, keep everything moving along. It isn't easy to connect with people when you're so connected to your burdens (weights that you can't do much about, anyway)! With the support of a persistent and patient wife and a good counselor, I was able eventually to take the load off of my back and lay it down in the back of the truck. God's way is so much easier!

Over the past few years, the more I have realized and accepted his love—just soaking it in like a sponge—the more I have been willing to trust him. In other words, since I have grown in my love for God, I have experienced greater trust in him thrown in as a bonus! The more I see that he has neither neglected nor forgotten me, the more I feel motivated to sign over bigger and bigger tracts of my life.

It is such a different way to live. Ever so slowly, like frost melting off a shadowed lawn in the warmth of the rising sun, trust has begun to replace fear. I am so grateful that I got in touch with God's deep, unwavering love for me so that I could trust him with more. And more and more and more.

All of this increased trust, of course, is simply a gift from him that I've finally had the good sense to receive. If he hadn't shown me and confirmed to me that he really was on my side, I don't think I ever could have fully trusted him with all the things I trust him with today.

How about you? Do you trust God more today than you did five years ago?

Some people have lived such terrible lives that they fear God's anger and don't totally trust him. Colossians 1:20-23 addresses this very issue: God speaks to us, telling us that through Christ, he has cleared a path into his presence. The price that Christ paid on the cross has made peace with God for the one who trusts in him. He says that many were far away from him, even to the point of being his enemy. Many were separated from him by their thoughts and actions, but God has brought them back as his friends.

When we trust in Christ, we are able to be in the presence of God with nothing held against us. The only requirement is that we fully believe that Christ died to save us and that we place our total trust in him. If we believe these things, we have no reason not to trust God with all that we have.

JACK'S TESTIMONY

Before I could trust God in a deeper way, I first had to admit I was afraid of him. My fear was not a healthy "fear of the Lord"—that deep, abiding respect and awe we feel in the presence of his majesty. It was more a matter of being afraid he would let me down or abandon me. I was scared of being hurt, scared of being disappointed, scared of having him walk out on me. Finally, I had to frankly face and admit those insecurities and fears. Before I could ever trust God, I had to first own up to the fact I was scared spitless of experiencing the sort of abandonment I had suffered in my childhood. It is hard for a man my size, who grew up in the gritty, tough neighborhoods of the housing projects, to openly admit he's insecure and fearful. Yet the very first step for someone like me to begin trusting God is to freely admit that persistent fear.

Where do you begin? You look into your Father's face and say, "Lord, you know my heart. I am insecure. I am afraid. And I give that to you. I need your touch. I admit that I am scared. I know what the Bible says and I believe it, but I'm still scared." Those are the times to say, along with David, "When I am afraid, I will trust in you" (Psalm 56:3).

When you truly trust God, you begin to do exactly what Jesus did. And that was to constantly seek the Father's face in prayer.

FACING THE WORST

Jesus was at it early, late, and in between. Mark gives us a snapshot of Christ's prayer life when he writes, "Very early in the morning, while it was still dark, Jesus got up, left the house and went off to a solitary place, where he prayed" (Mark 1:35). Jesus was always looking to his Father for direction, guidance, and companionship, and he did that through prayer.

As the years passed, Jesus spoke to his Father increasingly about the cross.

The book of Hebrews gives us this intimate glimpse into the God-man's life: "During the days of Jesus' life on earth, he offered up prayers and petitions with loud cries and tears to the one who could save him from death, and he was heard because of his reverent submission" (Hebrews 5:7).

A life full of trust, then, is a life full of prayer and seeking God. You can't maintain one without the other. And that kind of connection enables you to, just as Jesus did, imagine the worst outcome and yet consider even *that* worthy of the sacrifice. In Christ's life, the long, cold shadow of the cross loomed ahead of him. It was a horror to him, and his humanity shrank from it. Yet he understood that he had come to earth for that very purpose. As Isaiah prophesied, "And when he sees all that is accomplished by the anguish of his soul, he shall be satisfied; and because of what he has experienced, my righteous Servant shall make many to be counted righteous before God, for he shall bear all their sins" (Isaiah 53:11, TLB).

What's the worst that can happen to you and me? Knowing, as Paul assures us, that nothing in heaven, earth, or hell can ever separate us from the love of God that is in Christ Jesus our Lord—what's the *worst?* "Trouble or hardship or persecution or famine or nakedness or danger or sword?" (Romans 8:35). Those are all pretty tough circumstances. Yet what does Paul say? "No, in all these things we are more than conquerors through him who loved us" (verse 37).

So what's the worst that can happen? Death itself? Yet what is death but an instant ticket into God's presence? You begin to develop a deep sense of peace when you say to yourself, "No matter what happens, no matter if I have to face hurt, humiliation, poverty, or death itself, my life belongs to him. I am safe forever with him."

That's what made the martyrdom of teenager Cassie Burnall so powerful. In April 1999, two young men entered Columbine High School in Littleton, Colorado, and opened fire on their fellow students. The killers made their way toward the library, leaving a path of death and destruction in their wake.

When they arrived there, they found sixteen-year-old sophomore Cassie Burnall sitting at a table, reading her Bible. That in and of itself was a miracle, because Cassie had been a devoted follower of witchcraft before trusting Jesus with her life.

One of the gunmen pointed his automatic weapon at her head and asked if she believed in God. Cassie must have known what was coming. Yet after a moment's hesitation she looked calmly into the gunman's hate-hardened features and said, "Yes, I believe in God." As soon as she uttered those words, the killer laughingly asked, "Why?" then pulled the trigger, killing Cassie instantly.

Why indeed. You and I might ask the same question. Why trust in a God who does not step in and protect his sons and daughters from all evil? The truth is, believers are not immune to the hurts and hardships of life on this fallen planet. It's not a question of whether "bad things" will happen to you, because they will. The question is, What are the ultimate results? When Cassie trusted God even to the point of death, some amazing things began to happen…at Columbine High School…in Littleton, Colorado…and around the world.

Two girls who watched Cassie die came out of that library committed to never again compromise their faith. One girl led her entire soccer team to Christ, because if Cassie could stand for Jesus in death, she could stand for him in life. Kids all over America who heard the story of a young martyr their own age came to Christ or recommitted their lives to him. A revival among young and old alike was sparked by the courage of that young girl who completely trusted God with all she had. When Cassie's parents were interviewed about her death, they said that they could think of no greater honor than to have a child who was willing to trust her life to God, even at the point of death.

To me, that's not only trust on the part of Cassie, but tremendous trust on the part of her parents as well. They believe that, in some incomprehensible way, the horror at Columbine and their own painful loss will glorify

God and advance his kingdom; they believe that Cassie's death was a victory, not a defeat. That's a great sign of trust: the ability to envision the worst and to affirm that it is worth any sacrifice to walk in the will of God and fellowship of Jesus Christ.

What about Trusting Others?

Learning to trust God is one thing. Deep down, we know he is *trustworthy.* But we can't always say the same thing about people.

In fact, sometimes we trust others too much. Just because a person says he's a Christian, we may jump to the conclusion that he's worthy of our trust. Maybe he is…and maybe not! Trust needs to be earned. We shouldn't be foolish about trust and dispense it freely to anyone and everyone who wears the label "Christian." We need to be discerning. As Jesus said, "I am sending you out like sheep among wolves. Therefore be as shrewd as snakes and as innocent as doves. Be on your guard against men" (Matthew 10:16-17).

I remember hearing about a young Christian couple sitting in one of those "little white rooms" in a used-car dealership. The salesman haranguing them realized he wasn't making much progress, but he had noticed this was a churchgoing couple. So he called in the resident "Christian" salesperson. "Well, praise the Lord!" the man boomed as he walked beaming into the room. "Let's see what we can do for you here."

The couple bought the car but realized later that they had been taken by yet one more sales tactic. The man behind the hallelujahs was concerned only with racking up another sale. It is easy to understand why C. S. Lewis said his biggest problem with Christianity was Christians. His comment clearly expresses what so many of us feel and know: We are not very good at representing Jesus or the Christian faith. It is hard to trust even fellow Christians.

Even so, there comes a time when we have to acknowledge that *every* human relationship involves an element of risk. Because we have learned to trust God, we can also learn to trust others, knowing that if we are abandoned or rejected or if some individual proves unworthy of our trust, God will see us through even that situation. But many people, because they have been abandoned or abused by a parent, sibling, or spouse, have chosen to trust no one. Ever.

That sort of protection is in no way worth the price. Those who live behind such cold stone walls have secured a dubious safety at the cost of countless blessings. That's no way to live! In fact, it's really not living at all. When you trust someone and that trust is honored with reciprocal dedication and devotion, you gain great strength. Life becomes a richer tapestry, full of laughter, companionship, unexpected challenges, and unparalleled joy. If we never risk, never reach out, never make ourselves vulnerable to another, we die in isolation and spiritual immaturity.

Even though we have been "let down" or deceived by others, we can heal as we learn from those experiences. Eventually, we will be able to trust others again. Placing our trust in God allows us to trust others because we know that we do not have to allow ourselves to be victimized.

My inability to trust other people boiled down to not trusting God to take care of me. When I told myself I couldn't bear facing the possibility of being hurt or abandoned again, I was telling the Lord he couldn't handle such a situation. But he can! As Paul affirmed: "I have strength for all things in Christ Who empowers me [I am ready for anything and equal to anything through Him Who infuses inner strength into me]" (Philippians 4:13, AMP).

Sandy and I were discussing the early days of our relationship and marriage. We noted how different certain aspects of our union are today. Then, I was one of the most jealous men imaginable; I wanted to inspect what she wore to ensure it was not too provocative. I did not trust. Why? Because *I* was not trustworthy. Now, eighteen years later, we are discussing how free we both are. I feel no jealousy, no mistrust. Why not? Because today I truly trust God, and that trust has produced character where before it did not exist. Because I am more trustworthy, I can trust my wife and others.

Not trusting people is usually a symptom of not trusting God. Yes, when someone betrays you or abandons you, it hurts. And it's God's love that puts the salve on that hurt. But when I run from all relationships for fear of the cuts and bruises, I'm not trusting God that he'll give me that salve. David, the psalmist, did believe in God's salve. He wrote: "Though my father and mother forsake me, the LORD will receive me" (Psalm 27:10).

WHAT ABOUT FORGIVENESS?

A big part of trusting is forgiveness. People who cannot trust also have a hard time forgiving. Forgiveness is a final acknowledgment that I will not be able to change my past. Nothing that anybody says or does will change my past. So by forgiving someone, I'm accepting my past and the fact that I cannot change it. I am choosing to live in the present instead of a dead past. Shame from our past locks us into it. Grace for our past frees us for our future. Without God's gracious forgiveness through Jesus, shame becomes our inner guide back to a past that cannot be changed and a past that robs us of today and every day.

I met a young man at a conference who asked me a question that was tearing him apart. When he was two years old, his mother had taken him to a neighbor, left him, and never returned. Now that he was a young adult, his mother wanted to begin a relationship with him. He was still angry with her and had never resolved the pain of abandonment. Somehow the Lord gave me the right insight.

"Can you get in touch with her tonight"? I asked him.

"Yes," he replied, somewhat dubiously.

"Then that's what you need to do. And when you get in touch with her tonight, ask her about her own childhood. Have you ever come to understand what it was in her that would lead her to do what she did?"

The young man admitted he knew nothing of his mother's past and promised he would contact her. That evening he followed through and spoke with his remorseful mother. She told him a sad story. Very early in her own life, she, too, had been abandoned by her mother—left in a neighbor's home, just as he had been left. Only, in her case, her mother had never again tried to make contact. She simply walked out of her daughter's life forever. So this mother was actually trying to do something *beyond* what she had been taught. She was trying to restore the broken relationship.

My young friend returned to the conference the next day, spending most of his time in tears. He felt a new bond with his mother. He understood her struggle and her sorrow. And now he was able to trust her by making himself vulnerable.

Of course, learning to trust others does not always come easily. One broken woman, a victim of her father's sexual abuse, lost her ability to trust God or any other person. People would ask her to trust in Christ, but she could not allow herself to trust any male figure. Finally she began counseling sessions with a gentleman of integrity who had her best interests at heart. He guided her through her fears. He showed her that not all men are untrustworthy and that some are capable of caring with no strings attached. He also led her to trust in a God who loved her. Her faith had been poisoned by a man who had abused her, but it was restored and filled with trust by another who could be trusted.

Healthy believers are not naive, but they are able to place their trust in God, in others (who earn that trust), and even in themselves. They are not loners; they do not have to do everything themselves. They are willing to trust others with important tasks even though they know things might not turn out exactly as they'd like. They demonstrate by their actions that they believe in people. They do not allow their fears to turn them inward.

As our faith matures, our trust in God will grow. We will no longer sway with the whims of the day or run from a fear of others. Knowing that God will not betray us, we are freed to trust him, others, and ourselves.

Turning from Fear

It is sad that so many Christians are living in fear rather than living free. Many have accepted Christ as savior and are guaranteed a life in eternity with God. But here on earth their life is a living hell because they are unable to trust God with all that they are and do. They fear life will somehow spin out of control. They work hard at staying "in control," so the idea of turning everything over to God does not fit their way of doing things.

I can't help but think of the wealthy young man who came within an eyelash of finding eternal life in Christ. Full of earnest spiritual desire, he ran up to Jesus and fell on his knees before him. "Good teacher," he asked, "what must I do to inherit eternal life?" (Mark 10:17). He was willing to live a righteous life and keep all the commandments. But then Jesus placed his finger on the very area of his greatest struggle. The young man could not trust God with his finances.

Mark says, "Jesus looked at him and loved him. 'One thing you lack,' he said. 'Go, sell everything you have and give to the poor, and you will have treasure in heaven. Then come, follow me'"(verse 21). And how did the man respond? "At this the man's face fell. He went away sad, because he had great wealth" (verse 22).

There are many reasons people *say* they trust God but really don't. Some don't trust because of their need to control; others are controlled by some addiction or love of the world. Until each of these people see they are enslaved, they will never be able to trust God fully.

Where Are You?

If you are growing in a healthy faith, you entrust more of your life to God today than you did when your faith was new. Areas you thought you could not turn over to him, you do so anyway. For some it is a career; for others, a marriage. For many it is their money. Whatever we so tightly cling to is causing us to squeeze the life out of our faith.

If you are having a hard time trusting God, ask him to ease your fears. Ask him to heal your distrust. Then do your part. Look at the people who have betrayed you. Find out how much their influence affects your lack of trust. And do not allow those problems to rob you of a full relationship with God.

Then ask yourself, "What am I afraid of?" Examine your motives and explore what great things could come even if your worst fears were realized. Do whatever it takes to grow in your trust in God.

Make a bold move and trust God today. Surrender more and more to him. You will not be disappointed. Your trust will not spare you from the evils of the world, but it will protect you from a life without purpose. And under God's plan, every pain will have a purpose, and from every misery will come meaning and the opportunity to minister to others who also struggle.

CHAPTER 5

CALLED BY NAME

A Healthy Faith Is Personal

Fear not, for I have redeemed you; I have summoned you by name; you are mine.

Isaiah 43:1

I've often wondered about Nathanael. What was he thinking about on that lazy, soon-to-be-momentous afternoon under the shade of the fig tree? What did he ponder as he watched the majestic clouds sail across the blue vault of heaven?

Was he thinking about God? Was he wondering if the Almighty truly had any interest in or concern for someone as common and run-of-the-mill as he? What would the God of Abraham, Moses, David, Solomon, and Esther—the God of warriors and prophets and patriarchs and poets—have to do with a rather ordinary Israelite, sheltering himself from the heat of the day under a nondescript tree?

His question may have received the hint of an answer when his friend Philip came hurrying along the road, red-faced from the heat. The gospel of John picks up the story:

"Philip found Nathanael and told him, 'We have found the one Moses wrote about in the Law, and about whom the prophets also wrote—Jesus of Nazareth, the son of Joseph.'

" 'Nazareth! Can anything good come from there?' Nathanael asked.

" 'Come and see,' said Philip" (John 1:45-46).

Nathanael was about to experience a most personal encounter with the Messiah—and it would change forever any notion he might have had about an aloof, impersonal God. The Gospel writer picks up the details of the wondrous encounter:

"When Jesus saw Nathanael approaching, he said of him, 'Here is a true Israelite, in whom there is nothing false.'

" 'How do you know me?' Nathanael asked.

"Jesus answered, 'I saw you while you were still under the fig tree before Philip called you.'

"Then Nathanael declared, 'Rabbi, you are the Son of God; you are the King of Israel.'

"Jesus said, 'You believe because I told you I saw you under the fig tree. You shall see greater things than that'" (John 1:47-50).

Filled with great astonishment and awe, Nathanael understood that Jesus Christ had seen him and taken note of him when he was alone, perhaps pondering the mysteries of how an "insignificant" man could ever find a relationship with a vast and majestic God. The Lord knew Nathanael personally. And the Lord called him to a personal, intimate relationship with himself. *"I saw you while you were still under the fig tree. You shall see greater things than that!"*

When God calls a man, he calls him *personally.* When God calls a woman, he calls her *personally.* There is no group discount for entering his kingdom. Instead he tugs at the hearts of individuals, calling them one by one. It is the biblical pattern, repeated time and again.

From the time the Creator walked with Adam in the garden during the cool of the day, calling out to him by name after he rebelled, and right through the Old and New Testaments, we see a God who relates to men and women in a personal way. The examples are legion.

- The angel of the Lord called Hagar by name as she wandered hopelessly in a desert wilderness. Scripture says he "found Hagar near a spring in the desert; it was the spring that is beside the road to Shur. And he said, 'Hagar, servant of Sarai, where have you come from, and where are you going?'" (Genesis 16:7-8).

- The angel of the Lord appeared to an unimpressive young man named Gideon, who crouched in a winepress threshing wheat to avoid being seen by his Midianite enemies. "When the angel of the LORD appeared to Gideon, he said, 'The LORD is with you, mighty warrior'" (Judges 6:12).

- The Lord appeared to young Samuel, calling him by name again and again until the lad responded (1 Samuel 3).

- Jesus stopped at the fishing boat of Simon and Andrew as they were casting their nets, and said, "Come, follow me...and I will make you fishers of men" (Matthew 4:19).

- Jesus halted Saul of Tarsus in his tracks in the middle of the highway, calling him by name (Acts 9:1-9).

- An angel of the Lord called Philip the evangelist out of a booming citywide crusade in Samaria and plunked him down in the desert by the chariot of a seeking soul—an African eunuch—in order to lead that man to salvation and great joy (Acts 8:26-40).

And so it has been through the millennia. God has been calling not only a people but also individual men and women and boys and girls into a personal relationship with him. He did it in the Old Testament: "But now, this is what the LORD says—he who created you, O Jacob, he who formed you, O Israel: 'Fear not, for I have redeemed you; I have summoned you by name; you are mine'" (Isaiah 43:1). In the New Testament, Jesus compared such a relationship to a shepherd's intimate knowledge of his own flock. He knows every rascally ram, every timid ewe, and every frisky little lamb. He knows each of their peculiarities and habits. He knows which sheep follow the shepherd and which are inclined to walk over cliffs or into the mouths of lions. And when it comes time to move from one pasture to the next, "He calls his own sheep by name and leads them out. When he has brought out all his own, he goes on ahead of them, and his sheep follow him because they know his voice" (John 10:3-4).

Many people can read the Scriptures and know a lot about God, but that isn't the same as having an intimate relationship with God. In such a relationship we are able to share, identify, and surrender our individual weaknesses. On the other hand, in an impersonal, strictly knowledge-based relationship, the Scriptures become a set of rules and regulations to follow in order to avoid being punished.

In a healthy faith system, our relationship with God will manifest itself in a compassion for hurt and lost individuals. Our ability to empathize allows relationships to deepen and become intimate. We will be able to walk together, sharing our struggles as easily as our triumphs. Mercy, grace, and encouragement to do good works, along with personal presence and helping hands, replace the shaming, intolerant condemnation for the lost and backslidden so often present in a toxic system.

In a healthy faith system, the ability to restore wandering brothers or sisters and bear one another's burdens (Galatians 6:1-5) becomes not only a living reality, but also a way of life. Peter's admonition to clothe ourselves with humility toward one another (1 Peter 5:5-6) becomes the rule, rather than the exception.

A UNIQUE EXPERIENCE

As relationships within the family have declined, so has the understanding of a relationship with Father God. As divorced and working parents have spent less time with their kids, the concept of a personal God and Savior has faded.

Our ideas of God—fortunately or unfortunately—are often wrapped up in our experiences with our parents. An absent father is almost a guarantee for belief in an absent God, too busy to care about individuals. A passive father leaves children to wonder if God can or will become involved in their problems and day-to-day struggles. If your parents did not devote themselves to spending time with you, you probably began life feeling overwhelmed due to a lack of support. If you carried that experience over to God, your sense of feeling overwhelmed may have grown unmanageable. You may have broken down because you felt life was too difficult with too little support from a distant God.

The personal part of faith is the way I uniquely experience my relationship with God...the times I feel his nearness...the times I sense his heart yearning for my companionship...the times I know that I have grieved his Spirit because of something I have said or done...the times when his peace rolls over me like a Pacific breaker. Another person may feel something wholly different and may describe his or her relationship with Jesus in completely dissimilar terms. But that's what makes it *personal.*

So far as we know, the Lord had never before (and would never again) say to someone, "I saw you under the fig tree." Those words were meant for Nathanael alone, and they meant the world to him.

So far as we know, the resurrected Christ never knocked anyone else to the ground with a blinding, bright light from heaven and an audible voice that sounded like thunder. Yet that's what it took to reach Saul of Tarsus.

And how did he (or will he) reach you? How will he speak his love and his will into your ears? How will he work with you to maximize your personality and gifts to accomplish the work of his kingdom? I have no idea! That's the personal component of your relationship with him. A healthy faith develops in a personal way within the guiding parameters of God's Word.

The way I [Jack] experience my son is different from the way I experience my daughter. In each case it's personal. Those relationships are not the same. They're different. Not better or worse, not good or bad, just different. The way I love my son and daughter is very, very personal to me.

And so it is in my relationship with God; I relate to him and he relates to me in a very personal, particular matter. He doesn't speak to each of us with exactly the same tone of voice or approach us at exactly the same times or deal with us in exactly the same ways.

Sometimes I'll hear other parents say, "If I spoke to my firstborn the way I have to speak to my secondborn—just to make myself heard—it would *crush* him. Yet strong words seem to roll off the younger boy like water off a waxed car." In the same way, our heavenly Father speaks to his children (whom he knows so well) in very personal ways. He knows just the right amount of pressure to communicate his point to each person.

Whenever someone seeks to generalize your relationship with God— seeking to make it look, sound, taste, or feel just like some "approved, standardized" experience—you are treading close to the area of toxic faith.

Please hear this: It doesn't matter whether your belief matches someone else's in every respect. It doesn't matter that your experience of God's voice, God's presence, God's provision, God's tenderness, or God's discipline fails to line up with what others have told you about their experiences. It *should* be different (that is, within those unchanging biblical parameters). That's what a personal faith is all about!

HEALTHY CHURCHES ENCOURAGE PERSONAL FAITH

Healthy faith is a personal experience generated internally through trust in God, rather than being generated externally through rules made by other people. Each individual is personally led by the Holy Spirit. Each person can read God's Word and hear God speak through his Word. Christ died for each individual. *The healthier the faith becomes, the more personal it becomes.* A personal relationship forms between the believer and God. That relationship becomes so strong that no criticism or human-engineered system can break the personal bonds formed between God and a believer.

Unhealthy faith communities often teach an impersonal faith. Members are mere drones in the collective, not individuals loved and cherished by God. The entire system is based on the absence of personal convictions and the acceptance of someone else's definition of faith.

The true church needs to show men and women a God who wants to connect with them at the very point of their personal need. For instance, before Willow Creek Community Church was launched in the suburbs of Chicago, leaders began with an extensive canvassing of their community, seeking to determine what people liked and didn't like about church. They wanted to meet needs *within their community.* They wanted to bring people to the Lord by trying to address specific areas of spiritual hunger and distinct personal needs. So they tailored the music, worship style, teaching, drama, and small-group fellowships to meet the expressed desires of their community. The result is a story that's being told all over the world.

What takes place at Willow Creek, of course, is excellent for Willow Creek. Other communities have differing needs, just as the individuals within them differ. What works at Willow Creek may not translate to Minot, North Dakota. What meets needs in Naples, Florida, may not translate at all in Seattle. What's important is that the church break old community stereotypes and declare a God and Savior who deeply cares about the needs of individuals where they are. Since God loves individuals personally, the church needs to serve them personally and to do its best to speak to individual hurts and hopes and longings. The church that reflects Christ's earthly ministry will do just that, encouraging people to believe personally in Jesus, the Shepherd who knows each of his sheep by name.

Jesus really is the great counselor and comforter. He is large enough to know the needs of all and intimate enough to know your individual needs. Can you imagine if you went to a psychologist or a counselor and divulged your most personal problems? Can you imagine pouring out your life with all its hurts and fears? And then, can you imagine your counselor saying, "Well, this is what I tell all my clients." Wouldn't you be horribly offended? Or what if the counselor pulled out a textbook, looked up your problem, and then read some pat answer. Wouldn't you be upset? (If you were not upset, then you would really be in need of help!)

No one wants to be treated like a number or a case study. You want someone who knows you and can help you personally; that is what a counselor is for. You can get the other stuff from a computer! Jesus knows this. He does not treat you impersonally. He treats you as an individual.

A GOD BIG ENOUGH TO CARE ABOUT LITTLE ME

Those who do not believe in a personal God, in One who cares for individuals as well as groups, are missing out on a relationship that can make life bearable in the bad times and incredible in the good ones. God cares for people individually, and he will reveal himself to each of us if we allow him to do so.

One of the first persons to enter our New Life Treatment Centers was a confirmed atheist. One night he flew into a suicidal rage and out of desperation sought a phone book to find the number of a psychiatrist. At 3:00 A.M. few psychiatrists are available, but ours answered her phone. She instructed the desperate man to come to the center that night. He woke up the next morning and said that if there were a God, he had played a terrible trick by landing him in a Christian treatment center. It was tough for him to stay, but he struggled and managed to make it to the fourth day.

On the evening of the fourth day something remarkable happened. The man accompanied other alcoholic patients to an Alcoholics Anonymous meeting. At the end of the meeting, a young boy stood up and asked for help. He told them he was suicidal. He said he was visualizing, in full color, putting a gun to his head and pulling the trigger. The atheist could relate to the boy, since he had been in the same frame of mind four days earlier.

When the boy sat down, silence filled the room. Suddenly, the back door of the room opened and a man walked in wearing what looked like a turban and a hospital robe. He said that his wife and kids were in the car, but he felt God wanted him to come into the room and say something. He had not heard the boy but said, "If anyone here is thinking of killing yourself, I want to encourage you to reconsider. God loves you and wants you to live. This turban on my head is a bandage from where I put a gun to my head and pulled the trigger. Fortunately, I survived so I could come here and tell you not to do it. God loves you."

That day our atheist patient lost his atheism. He believed God had sent that man to talk to that boy. The other patients believed God had sent the boy *and* the man to show the atheist that he is a real God. I believe God interrupted the natural course of events to build the faith of all in that room and potentially all who read this story.

This is but one of millions of stories about men and women who have met a personal God who is not too big to care about each individual. If he knows all the stars and calls each by name (Psalm 147:4; Isaiah 40:26), is it too much to believe that he knows and cares about each one of us? In a thousand ways, through good times and bad, God has tried to make himself known through meeting personal needs. Who cannot point to instances where God's divine intervention makes a more logical explanation than mere coincidence? Our agnostic society encourages us to explain events in any way except that God stepped in. We search the universe for God, but all the time he is with us. He is in love with each of us and cares for us individually. Just as Jesus saw Nathanael—and the contents of his heart—when that seeking soul was sitting under a fig tree, so he sees you and reads the content of your heart in your present situation, wherever it might be.

He's a big enough God to do that.

He's a personal enough God to do that.

He's a loving enough God to do that.

CHAPTER 6

NOTHING TO PROVE

A Healthy Faith Is Confident of God-Given Value

I am not in the least inferior to the "super-apostles," even though I am
nothing.

2 Corinthians 12:11

Here's a paradox for you.

Someone with a healthy sense of self may be the best candidate to exercise true humility. Why? He has nothing to prove. No agenda to push. No fragile ego to shield at all costs. And he doesn't waste his time fretting over what other people think of him. When he encounters a question that exceeds his knowledge, he has no problem shrugging his shoulders and saying, "Great question. I really don't know the answer." He doesn't feel as though he *has* to have all the answers.

Sometimes we believers fool ourselves into thinking that, since God has all knowledge and wisdom and since we have his Holy Spirit within us, we should be able to dispense pearls of wisdom like spiritual gumballs. But that's the height of arrogance. The truth is, the more we come to know God, the more we realize what we don't know. And that's just fine! The more we experience the work of his Spirit within us, the lower we will bow before God's throne, admitting our utter dependence upon him.

Job experienced that reality as perhaps no one else in history. As one of the most prominent men of his day, he might have thought he had a pretty good handle on theology. Yet after God swept the patriarch along on a "magical mystery tour" of creation and all its wonders, that good man could only stammer: "I know that you can do all things; no plan of yours can be thwarted.... Surely I spoke of things I did not understand, things too wonderful for me to know.... My ears had heard of you but now my eyes have seen you" (Job 42:2,3,5). With that, Job bowed low in humble worship.

Here was a man who realized afresh that he did not have all the answers—nor even very many of them. But he had seen the Lord's mighty hand up close and personal, and that was enough to fill his cup to overflowing.

"ALL THE ANSWERS"?

Whenever I [Jack] think of someone who doesn't have to know all the answers, my mind invariably turns to my friend, Ron Wright. An associate professor of theology at Vanguard University of Southern California, Ron is a very learned man with a healthy grasp of the Scriptures. He's probably forgotten more than I'll ever know about the Bible. Yet for all his knowledge and learning, he has no problem admitting that he might be in error. He gives his classes the fruit of his extensive, diligent studies and works hard to provide astute biblical reasons for his positions.

But that doesn't mean he's seen all the angles.

That doesn't mean he's always right.

And he's okay with that.

Ron doesn't *need* to be right every time. He can express an opinion, and his ego doesn't demand that you agree with it. Maybe that's why people always feel so comfortable when they're around him. He has such a warm and winning way of hearing contrary points of view without taking them as competition or a challenge to his authority. He can present his view confidently and persuasively without being arrogant or condescending. He has a wonderful ability to examine someone else's perspective and disagree with it, without ever making that individual feel demeaned or vilified.

At times those skills have been put to a severe test! Ron once taught a Sunday school class attended by a former marine. The man was never shy about speaking his mind, and when it came to biblical issues, he espoused a take-no-prisoners attitude.

Ron was very gentle and tactful whenever this brother got into his take-that-hill mode. Our military friend would loudly insist, "We need to do this and we need to do that," as if this "we" were a calling upon the whole church. Ron would gently explain there might be another way of looking at it. In a respectful, noncondemning manner, he pointed out how our friend's casehardened positions could be at odds with the wider scope of Scripture.

While some in the class may have been crawling in their chairs and gritting their teeth when this gentleman barked forth his opinions, Ron never seemed discomfited. With an affirming smile, he was able to refocus the class without humiliating or shaming the man.

That's the mark of a truly humble person—someone who is comfortable inside his own skin and confident in his position as a child of God, a man who teaches what he has learned but stays open to correction or differing points of view.

WE ARE VALUABLE TO GOD

The truth is, the healthier our faith, the more valuable we can feel. Too often we base our self-worth on what the world views as valuable. The world thinks money is the barometer of value, and if we do not have it in great amounts, we feel bad about ourselves. Physical beauty has almost become a religion unto itself, and those without it feel no value in a society that judges by the looks on the outside. In this age of technology, IQ is often used to determine who is to be esteemed and who is to be shown the basement.

It is difficult for most of us to measure up. And the more we focus on the world's standards and values, the more negative we feel about ourselves.

God has a different system, and if our faith is in him, we can feel tremendous relief. Christ talked about the worth of an individual. His words are good news to all of us who will never be fashion models, billionaires, or members of Mensa. Christ told his followers not to be afraid of those who attack a person physically, because the attackers cannot touch a person's soul. He explained that even though sparrows were sold for about a half cent each, not one sparrow can fall to the ground without God's knowing it. "So don't be afraid," he said, "you are worth more than many sparrows" (Matthew 10:31). The Greek word translated "you are worth more" is from the verb *diaphero,* which literally means "to excel, to be highly valued."

Now, if God knows the destinies of all the sparrows and cares about each one of them, we can feel wonderful about ourselves, knowing he cares much more for us. If our sense of self-worth is derived from God, we don't have to worry about what the world thinks of us or does to us. The fact that God sent his Son to die for us should be an overwhelming affirmation of the worth of each individual.

The problem comes when we measure ourselves by the world's standards and rely on our own efforts to measure up. Healthy faith stays focused on God and the value he has given each of us—first in our lofty status as beings made in his image and second as men and women redeemed by the precious blood of Christ. In the Creator's value system, no one need feel disappointment over not measuring up to the world. The person with a healthy faith *feels* valuable to the Creator because he or she *is* valuable to the Creator.

Scripture as a Club

Here is yet another irony. Those who struggle most with self-condemnation, who so deeply need the help and hope of the Scriptures, tend to use the Bible as a club with which to beat themselves. Words of condemnation and chastisement seem to jump off the pages at them as though in bold print and italics.

Through my [Jack's] years of ministry, my expertise has been in the area of sexual addiction. Those who struggle with this oh-so-vulnerable area of life will often take passages of Scripture out of context to "prove" to themselves (again and again) what worthless and wormlike creatures they are. Rather than seeing the many, many verses of hope and help and deliverance and forgiveness, they choose to interpret every passage in ways that increase their despair and self-loathing.

Sometimes young men will condemn themselves for simply being human. Someone will tell me, "I was down at the beach, I saw this pretty girl in a bathing suit, and I responded." Well *of course* he did! (He would have more to worry about if he didn't respond at all.) Males are designed to respond sexually. It is no sin when a young man sees a pretty woman on the beach and his blood pressure elevates, his eyes dilate, and he may or may not have an erection. That's simply how God made healthy males. But because of what momentarily passes through their minds (even though they rejected lingering thoughts), some young men feel depraved and worthless—forgetting the imputed worth and righteousness they have in Christ.

I think we need to keep in balance two equally accurate perspectives on ourselves. On the one hand, healthy believers hasten to agree with the apostle Paul that "nothing good lives in me, that is, in my sinful nature" (Romans 7:18). They know their sin and can feel, as Paul did, that they are "the worst of sinners" (1 Timothy 1:16). Yet they also know they have been redeemed by God and have been made into "a chosen people, a royal priesthood, a holy nation, a people belonging to God" (1 Peter 2:9). They understand that while their "old nature" is corrupt, it is also true that "if anyone is in Christ, he is a new creation; the old has gone, the new has come!" (2 Corinthians 5:17). So they can humbly make statements like the one Paul issued in 2 Corinthians 12:11: "I am not in the least inferior to the 'super-apostles,' even though I am nothing." To embrace both their fallenness and their redemption enables them to live with confidence and joy.

God already knows we fall short. Our struggle with unredeemed flesh is no surprise to him. His job, and his particular delight, is to pick us up and hold our hand as we grow. David had the right idea in Psalm 130:3-4: "If You, LORD, should mark iniquities, O Lord, who could stand? But there is forgiveness with You, that You may be feared" (NASB).

In other words, God realizes that no one would be able to fear and worship him if he had not provided a means of forgiveness and reconciliation. If he stood over every person waving a list of sins in each face, no one would ever worship God. But in his compassion and love, he has provided forgiveness through the sacrifice of his Son. Once we accept that provision and avail ourselves of daily self-examination and cleansing, we can put self-condemnation where it belongs…at the foot of the cross.

THE PROBLEM WITH "SPIRITUAL GIANTS"

Sometimes we conclude that God has called a few believers into service—the ministers—while the rest of us are assigned second-class status. So rather than ministering to others' needs, we pass on that task to those who have a "special calling" to do so. We also may feel that because we are such terrible sinners, God cannot use us anyway. Thus we fail to receive the blessings that come from ministering because we believe God uses only the perfect, the near perfect, or those he called into ministry.

In my life, as well as in Scripture, I have seen nothing but the opposite to be true. God often uses those who have major flaws or who have been through a great deal of pain to accomplish many vital tasks for his kingdom. Look at Moses the stutterer, Paul with his thorn in the flesh, and David the adulterer. It seems clear that God uses men and women despite their flaws.

No one is too messed up for God to use, and no task is too unimportant to matter to God. On the sidelines and in the lower levels of the organizations where the very visible ministers work, hundreds of faithful behind-the-scenes believers do the invaluable, powerful work of prayer, laying the foundation for greatness in organizations as well as in people. When people pray, God unleashes his power, people change, countries develop new political systems, and miracles occur.

Everyone has some gift granted by God that can be exercised in a mighty way. When we cultivate our talents, we will accomplish greater things than we ever imagined possible. When we do not develop our gifts, chances are we will never be satisfied or fulfilled. Some of us could never speak in front of fifty people, but we may feel comfortable teaching a Sunday school class of five. Year after year we teach, not knowing our long-term impact. Although our contributions may seem small, God is using us to lay a foundation for years of future service.

ON EQUAL FOOTING

How narrow-minded we earthbound believers can be! We tend to think that just because we value and honor TV preachers over prayer warriors, God does so also. We create a hierarchy of talents and gifting and then project our list onto God. What arrogance! A healthy faith flourishes in an environment of harmony, not hierarchy. The fact that individual ministries are different does not imply a difference in their moral worth. We're the ones who assign such values, not God.

Sometimes people in highly visible ministries will adopt the word "anointed" to give the impression that they have risen several notches above the average believer. Does anointing go hand in hand with celebrity, with being in the public spotlight? Who would be the *real* Christian heroes in a community if God had his say? Unless I miss my guess, it wouldn't be the guy strutting around on some platform in an Armani suit, who arrived in a limousine after flying across the nation in a private Lear jet from his beachfront mansion within his gated community. I'm not saying that such a person couldn't be a hero, but if I were a betting man, I'd put my money on a person like the man I met when I was speaking at a crisis pregnancy center recently.

This man pastors three small churches, none of which number over fifty. He preaches to all three congregations on both Sunday mornings and Wednesday evenings. The combined contributions of these three churches aren't enough to live on, so he also works another job.

He'll never have a radio broadcast or a tape ministry or be invited to anyone's talk show. No Christian publishers are hanging around his door, offering to take him to lunch at a fancy restaurant. If you ask *Who's Who* about this man, they'll say, "Who's he?" He's certainly no spiritual giant from earth's point of view…but in heaven? Who can say? Only the Chief Shepherd himself can put an appropriate value on the humble services of this faithful undershepherd. Eternity will reveal many surprises, and as Jesus stated so plainly, "But many who are first will be last, and many who are last will be first" (Matthew 19:30).

MEMBERS OF GOD'S HOUSEHOLD

Why then should you and I feel that we have value?

Because we have been invited to come into God's presence and kneel before his very throne. Hebrews 4:16 tells us, "Therefore let us draw near with confidence to the throne of grace, so that we may receive mercy and find grace to help in time of need" (NASB).

Because he has named us as fellow citizens of heaven along with the saints and members of God's own family. Ephesians 2:19-20 says, "You are no longer foreigners and aliens, but fellow citizens with God's people and members of God's household, built on the foundation of the apostles and prophets, with Christ Jesus himself as the chief cornerstone."

Because God chose us in Christ before the foundation of the world and adopted into his very family. "For he chose us in him before the creation of the world to be holy and blameless in his sight. In love he predestined us to be adopted as his sons through Jesus Christ, in accordance with his pleasure and will—to the praise of his glorious grace, which he has freely given us in the One he loves. In him we have redemption through his blood, the forgiveness of sins, in accordance with the riches of God's grace that he lavished on us with all wisdom and understanding" (Ephesians 1:4-8).

"But you don't know my track record!" someone will say. "You have no idea what sins I've committed and how I have presumed on the grace of God!"

True enough. But let's just carry that line of thinking a bit further. Think of the worst sin you can imagine. What would that be for you? In my mind, the "worst sin" would be a man who would kidnap, torture, rape, then murder an innocent child. Is that a horrible enough sin for you? The amazing thing is that anyone who has committed even that kind of heinous crime is still loved by God. Jesus died on the cross and paid the price for sins as heinous as those. God loves the worst, the most vile of us all.

Imagine this. Your name is Peter and you are known as "the Rock." When the Holy Spirit comes after Jesus ascends into heaven, you will be the one chosen to preach the sermon that will set the world on its ear. Your words will be heard in many languages and you will plant the seeds for a Christian church that will spread across the whole world. This is your destiny!

But before all that, you spend time with the Savior of the universe. You love him so much that when he wants to wash your feet, you try to refuse. If there had been a Jesus fan club in that day, you would have been the founder and president. You love him and following him is an unspeakable honor. When the end nears, Jesus lets you in on a little secret: You will become a fair-weather follower—in fact, a betrayer. You are aghast! You probably wonder if Jesus realizes the depths of your love for him.

Yet the fact is (if you had been Peter) you would have done exactly what Jesus predicted. You would have denied you ever knew him, much less followed him. And when you had finished distancing yourself from the One who was dying to save you, your shame would have been nearly unbearable. Washed up would have been much too kind a term. You might well have wondered if there was still a place for you in heaven.

Yet when Jesus rose from the grave, he made sure you were one of the first to hear the news. While he was dying, you were denying; yet when he arose, he still was thinking of you, still loving you. If you had been Peter, Jesus would have known your weakness, forgiven you for it, and come looking for you after his resurrection. Why? *Because he loved you and wanted to be with you and wanted to assure you that you were still a key player on heaven's team.*

Peter struggled to accept a love so loyal, so deep, so enduring. And so do you and I! You may know that nothing is supposed to be able to separate you from God's love, but the one thing you do not *feel* is loved. In fact, you feel that God loves everybody but you. You think you have done something too horrible for him to forgive. But in the face of your fear and alienation is a God who loves you so much that if you were the only person alive, he would have died *just for you.* That is no exaggeration.

IT BELONGS TO YOU

If your church does not teach such truths about God's unfathomable grace and love, it is critical for you to find a church that does! If all you hear is what a worm you are in the eyes of God, then—hear me, friend—you are not hearing a balanced message. How can any of us hate and devalue ourselves when God "did not spare his own Son, but gave him up for us all"? (Romans 8:32). I hope and pray that you can come to accept this divine mystery of how much God loves you just as you are, unworthy, yet deeply valued. Unable to earn the love but knowing there is no need to earn it.

All you have to do is accept it. Don't be like those who know of God's love but have never experienced it. Experience it!

For it belongs to you.

CHAPTER 7

PASSIONATE WITHOUT APOLOGY

A Healthy Faith Is Able to Embrace Human Emotions

We despised him and rejected him—a man of sorrows, acquainted with bitterest grief. We turned our backs on him and looked the other way when he went by.

Isaiah 53:3, TLB

If Jesus attended your church this Sunday, would he be shunned, criticized, or quietly avoided because of his open displays of emotion? Would you and I feel, well, a little uncomfortable—maybe a tad embarrassed—in the presence of such strong, spontaneous expressions as his anger at the temple money-changers or his grief at the spiritual condition of Jerusalem?

In many churches, I think there is a good chance he would be shamed or taken to task for such conduct.

"Get a grip on yourself, Jesus."

"Have you been saved, Jesus? Christians oughta be the happiest people on earth."

"Come on, Jesus—where is your faith?"

"Don't you know that Scripture says to 'rejoice always'?"

"You need to claim God's peace about this."

"You need to rebuke the demon of sadness."

"Give it to God, Jesus."

"Just praise the Lord anyway."

"Remember, Jesus, 'all things work together for good.'"

"If you must carry on like that, you should step back into the narthex. You're disrupting the service!"

"Smile, Jesus. God loves you and has a wonderful plan for your life."

Can't you just hear such comments being made—or at least muttered under someone's breath? Some of us might feel Jesus really didn't live up to our image of a "true man of God." The Son of God himself would likely be criticized for not "snapping out of it" or "having enough faith."

The truth is, of course, his faith was off the charts. In fact, Jesus had *perfect* faith and was absolutely sinless. Yet he allowed himself to experience the heights and depths of human emotion. He knew the mountaintops of great joy and the blackest chasms of depression and sorrow. He did not suppress his anger, choke off his tears, or mask his depression. And he did not fear to speak forth the deepest longings of his heart.

He was "a man of sorrows and acquainted with grief" (Isaiah 53:3, NASB). He was (and is) passionate without apology.

OUR PASSIONATE GOD

Throughout Scripture, God is revealed to be a passionate God. Some of us may not be comfortable with that. Others might seek to explain it away: "It's just a Hebrew, cultural thing." But our discomfort doesn't alter the facts one iota.

In the Old Testament we see glimpses of a God who possesses deep wells of passion. Through the prophet Jeremiah, he declares, "I have loved you with an everlasting love" (Jeremiah 31:3).

In the book of Hosea, he agonizes over the fate of rebellious Israel. You can almost catch a sob in his voice: "How can I give you up, O Ephraim? How can I surrender you, O Israel? How can I make you like Admah? How can I treat you like Zeboiim? My heart is turned over within Me, all My compassions are kindled" (Hosea 11:8, NASB).

That word "kindled" comes from a Hebrew root that can mean "to shrivel with heat." What a picture! This is no cool, dispassionate deity calmly observing the struggles of his children from the comfort of some easy chair among the clouds.

Can you hear the groan of a heartbroken parent when God says of Israel, "All day long I have held out my hands to an obstinate people, who walk in ways not good, pursuing their own imaginations—a people who continually provoke me to my very face" (Isaiah 65:2-3)?

OUR PASSIONATE FOREBEARS

The psalmists inherited their heavenly Father's strong passions. In fact, Psalms is a veritable textbook of emotional expression. Try telling David he should "be more reserved"! He wrote: "I am worn out from groaning; all night long I flood my bed with weeping and drench my couch with tears. My eyes grow weak with sorrow; they fail because of all my foes" (Psalm 6:6-7). At another low point in his life, David penned these words: "Be merciful to me, O LORD, for I am in distress; my eyes grow weak with sorrow, my soul and my body with grief. My life is consumed by anguish and my years by groaning.... I am forgotten by [my friends] as though I were dead; I have become like broken pottery" (31:9-10,12). Another psalmist admitted: "My tears have been my food day and night" (42:3).

At other times, this hymnbook of Israel is filled with raucous cymbal clashing, horn blasting, and mighty shouts of overflowing joy. A little excessive, you say? A little undignified, you protest? But what are we going to do with it? This sort of emotion flows through the pages of Scripture like a fast-running stream.

THE EMOTIONS OF A PERFECT MAN

When Christ walked the earth, he expressed his emotions freely and without shame. It's too bad so few of us choose to follow his example.

The Christian must recognize that Christ did not deny, suppress, or stuff his feelings; he embraced them. As he walked the earth, he revealed his love, anger, sorrow, and many other emotions. Beyond any question, he felt the depths of emotion.

Isn't that what makes Hebrews 4:15 such an encouraging passage? The writer reminds us that "we do not have a high priest who is unable to sympathize with our weaknesses." Jesus experienced everything that we do. Every emotion. Every temptation. The high highs, the low lows, and the flat in-betweens. He is One who understands what we feel *experientially.* Sometimes it's frustrating trying to describe to a counselor or friend what's going on in our heart—when we're not half sure what's happening ourselves. But Jesus 1knows. He doesn't have to guess or imagine. He *knows.*

John 11:35 is probably the only verse in Scripture short enough for me to memorize. But it's a good one, a text that has encouraged countless people down through the centuries. "Jesus wept." He is a God who feels. He knows the depths of our emotions, for he experienced them himself.

Luke describes how the Lord Jesus was stirred as he approached the city of Jerusalem for the final time. When he "saw the city, he wept over it and said, 'If you, even you, had only known on this day what would bring you peace—but now it is hidden from your eyes'" (Luke 19:41-42). How many times have you and I said something like that? *Oh, if only! If only it could have been different! If only...* Jesus grieved over Israel's lost opportunities.

Everything in his heart wanted to gather these rebellious people into his arms, but they continually turned away.

At Gethsemane, Jesus felt a heaviness of soul akin to death itself. Taking along his three closest companions—Peter, James, and John—he staggered into the depths of that olive orchard in the shadows of night. He said to his friends, "My soul is overwhelmed with sorrow to the point of death. Stay here and keep watch with me" (Matthew 26:38).

When Jesus prayed, "Let this cup pass from me" (verse 39, NASB), he was experiencing deep emotional conflict, not succumbing to sin. Just because our will and God's will may be in conflict from time to time, it is not necessarily sin; that's a reality. It's what we do with that conflict and how we resolve it that's important. And the fact that we might have some type of emotional expression as we resolve these issues is not sin—it's part of our humanity.

WHAT ABOUT ANGER?

Despite what you may have been taught, even anger can be a legitimate emotional response to our broken world.

Christ became angry, expressed it, and did something about it. His anger led him to cleanse the temple of money-changers. Without it, he would never have removed these violators of the temple's sanctity. The temple's money-changers and merchandisers did not have God at heart, but rather the profits they could earn from buying livestock low and selling it high. Christ knew their hearts and was hurt and angry over their presumption, dishonesty, and hypocrisy.

Mark relates an incident that occurred in a synagogue. The text says that "a man with a shriveled hand was there. Some of them were looking for a reason to accuse Jesus, so they watched him closely to see if he would heal him on the Sabbath. Jesus said to the man with the shriveled hand, 'Stand up in front of everyone.' Then Jesus asked them, 'Which is lawful on the Sabbath:

to do good or to do evil, to save life or to kill?' But they remained silent" (Mark 3:1-4).

What a terrible silence that was! It reeked with hypocrisy, hatred, jealousy, and a stubborn refusal to believe. The text says, "He looked around at them in anger and, deeply distressed at their stubborn hearts, said to the man, 'Stretch out your hand.' He stretched it out, and his hand was completely restored" (verse 5).

Now Jesus knew very well what sort of world he would enter when he stepped through the gates of heaven to be conceived in the womb of a teenage girl and born in Bethlehem. He was under no illusions about the intransigence, cruelty, hatred, and woodenheaded obstinacy he would encounter during his earthly sojourn. He knew very well that the sins of earth would cost him his life. Even so, when he came nose to nose with such sin and stubbornness in his teaching ministry, it caused him deep frustration— even to the point of burning anger.

What then does Scripture have to say about anger in our lives? It can certainly be sinful and out of control, even dangerous. But it doesn't have to be. The Bible gives us guidelines for expressing that anger in a healthy way. Paul writes: "'In your anger do not sin.' Do not let the sun go down while you are still angry, and do not give the devil a foothold" (Ephesians 4:26-27). What great counsel! Yes, you and I will experience surges of anger from time to time. And that anger is not necessarily sinful. The key lies in dealing with that anger before it finds a place to lodge and take root in our hearts. We need to deal with relational problems right away and not allow them to fester or seethe within us. That is where Satan finds a foothold in our lives.

James reminds us to be "slow to become angry." Why? Because "man's anger does not bring about the righteous life that God desires" (James 1:19-20). In other words, anger should not dominate our lives so that we're living with a perpetual chip on our shoulder, ready to fly off the handle at the slightest provocation. But neither James nor Paul says we should never be angry.

Of course, in some expressions of the Christian faith, anger is a no-no for both men and women. Some believe that everyone must be completely nice and pleasant at *all* times and that anyone showing anger is not a good Christian; he or she should work on the sinful attitude at the heart of the anger. But such a belief distorts how Christianity and reality are to be joined. Everyone, Christian or not, is going to get angry. The sooner this anger is expressed and resolved, the better. Yet many angry Christians don't acknowledge they are angry, even as they seethe with bitterness and resentment. Their denial of their feelings is both ineffective and unnecessary.

Without our anger we are unable to cleanse the temple of God and maintain its sanctity. Without our anger, we cannot get those people who violate the sanctity of our beings out of our lives. Without our anger, we are relegated to playing the role of enabler and victim.

Anger can be a mechanism for self-defense; those who deny its presence are vulnerable to manipulation and all forms of exploitation. People who don't have the right to be angry become powerless, unable to stand for what is right.

I can think of times when deliberately shoving back my anger resulted in an unhealthy long-term situation. Many years ago, I had a relationship with a wonderful girl I wanted to marry. When I caused the relationship to end through my own foolishness, I should have grieved and expressed my anger and rage at myself until I rid myself of every ounce of the venomous emotions. Instead I lived with self-anger and self-hatred, masking them with depression and long bouts of profound sadness.

Many people live with their negative feelings, as I did, rather than express them. Then they retreat to less negative feelings in an attempt to cope.

Some of us are walking paradoxes: The emotions we are willing to show don't match what we are actually feeling. We are in a constant state of denial when it comes to our emotions. Women, though angry on the inside, feel safe only if they show their misery and depression. Men, feeling sad and depressed, will not risk being labeled weak by expressing their sadness. So they mask their depression by pushing people around through their anger. An angry female without her depression could not exist. A depressed man without his anger could not cope. Both become addicted to the emotion that appears to be more tolerable and acceptable.

WOMEN WHO CAN'T BE ANGRY

In our society it's not considered ladylike to be angry, so many women were never allowed to express anger as little girls. Getting angry would have meant risking the wrath or perceived loss of love and attention of their parents. To be pleasing to a power greater than themselves (their parents), these women-to-be had to sacrifice their anger.

Without their anger, however, they cannot set boundaries and protect themselves from the violations that occur in life. Without their anger, they become victims to be violated, beaten, battered, and bruised. Without their anger, they cannot muster the courage to address their God. No matter how intense their rage at their plight in life, they cannot protect themselves or get the victimizers out of their lives. Their role is to be pleasing—and angry people are not pleasing.

Instead of expressing deep hurt, the wounded female lives a miserable existence and gripes and complains about everything. She becomes addicted to her misery because it allows her to forget about her anger (or at least postpone dealing with it). Her dependency on misery is just as difficult to break as someone else's dependency on crack cocaine. Both are a means to a different reality that allows for pain to be deferred.

MEN WHO CAN'T BE SAD

In our culture, it often seems more acceptable for men to be angry than to be sad. So we stumble through life without understanding our feelings, completely out of touch with our emotions. We are deeply grieved by our unrealized expectations and sense of inadequacy, but we don't feel safe acknowledging our sadness. We show our anger but never the deep hurt and sadness underneath it.

When we feel sad, anger becomes a safe retreat. It causes the adrenaline to rush through us. The payoff is not just that we avoid looking weak, but that we also feel different because of the chemicals coursing through our bodies. The more adrenaline we pump in anger, the less sadness we are forced to feel. However, this lack of grieving poisons us.

Of course, the Bible offers no precedent for men suppressing their deepest hurts and sorrows. The Old Testament depicts many real men showing their real emotions. The men of Israel would rip their clothes, sprinkle themselves with ashes, wear black armbands, and spend time in mourning and grief. They would wail before the Lord to process their shame and pain. That extremely freeing experience allowed them to express their emotions to the full degree and then move on without the baggage of negative feelings. Without the ability to wail before the Lord, we are forced to repress our disappointments and sadness and find ways to compensate for these emotions by replacing them with others less threatening.

HEALTHY CHURCHES, HEALTHY SAINTS

Healthy faith affirms passionate emotion; unhealthy faith denies people the chance to feel what they really feel. Healthy churches are healing centers where we can express our true feelings as well as find prayer support, accountability, appropriate forgiveness, and cleansing. Unhealthy churches are peopled with plastic saints who look good, say all the right things, and support an image of perfectionism. Every problem must be wiped away with a quick "Praise the Lord!" Real feelings are abandoned for the "good" ones supporting the myth that the truly faithful are free of problems. After all, revealing problems or struggles would indicate weakness and a lack of faith!

Leaders in unhealthy churches or organizations don't want to face the reality of human needs, either their own or those of other people. They want to live in a world where everything can be fixed with a great sermon or a quick prayer. The illusion that allows the organization to grow, the family to look good, and the leader to continue to be out of touch with people and their needs takes precedence over real needs and real feelings.

Genuine, healthy Christianity, however, is able to embrace who we are as human beings. God knows your struggles, your heartache, your brokenness. He does not reject you because you have needs or feel strong flashfloods of emotion. Instead, he wants to point you to godly resources to meet those needs...and ultimately, to himself. *He made you.* Who understands you better than he? God created us as emotional beings. He created us with needs. The key is that he wants every one of those needs to point us back to him.

The ability to show genuine emotion is a hallmark of a healthy, growing faith. Zombielike responses to human tragedy or pain do not grow out of an authentic faith, but often are symptomatic of toxic belief. Genuine Christian experience encourages believers to "rejoice with those who rejoice; mourn with those who mourn" (Romans 12:15). It validates and honors the whole range of human emotion.

In healthy faith there is no need to hide our feelings. We can rejoice that God has given us emotions by which to experience the extremes of life. We should acknowledge them, confess them when they are based on a wrong view of God, and express them as they develop.

Healthy faith allows us to embrace all aspects of our humanity. It acknowledges our capacity to sin and make mistakes. There is no illusion of perfection, no need to be perfect or to hide when we fail. Healthy faith allows us to experience God's mercy and grace...and pass it along. As Paul noted, we who experience suffering and hurt and then feel the comfort of Christ are the ones best qualified to administer first aid to others.

We become wounded healers. Just like Jesus.

He Is There!

When we suffer, many times we want Christ to relieve the pain. That's only natural. I had a root canal done yesterday. Unfortunately for me, the root was so thick they could not deaden it with painkillers. So I had to endure what seemed like an hour or more of wrenching pain. The Lord would have loved to prevent that suffering, but we live in a fallen world, and *there will be pain.* There will be sadness. There will be disappointment and loneliness and grief and anger and fear.

But when we suffer any or all of these things, he is there!

He has been where we are, and he walks with us and weeps with us. And with your tears he can water the seeds of character planted by pain. So rather than reject these feelings, embrace them, because the Lord is embracing you.

CHAPTER 8

THE REAL DEAL

A Healthy Faith Is Vulnerable

He took Peter and the two sons of Zebedee along with him, and he began
to be sorrowful and troubled. Then he said to them, "My soul is overwhelmed with sorrow to the point of death. Stay here and keep watch
with me."

Matthew 26:37-38

In 1994 God did an amazing thing in my life that propelled me into the
homes, businesses, and cars of people all over America. I had started New Life
Treatment Centers in 1988, providing Christ-centered treatment to those
suffering from severe emotional and addiction problems. God blessed our
organization and we grew rapidly. In 1993 Frank Minirth and Paul Meier of
the Minirth Meier Clinics talked to me about acquiring their organization.
Since they had not only treatment centers, but outpatient clinics as well, we
could address people's needs at every level.

With this acquisition came a nationwide radio broadcast. As head of the
new organization, I had the job of taking that program to the next level. In
the past the show had been filled with psychology and psychiatry; I wanted
to fill it with more Scripture. I wanted to show that the Bible speaks to the
issues that confront us all. So I began to give the show a more biblical format.
But something else also needed to be done.

The show needed to be more *real.*

It needed to reflect Scripture, not merely what is seen and heard on many other Christian television and radio programs. I believed that if we were to reach a new and younger audience, our listeners would have to perceive that we were living out our faith in the midst of our failures and struggles. And I was convinced I had to lead the way. As scary as that would be, I would have to step out and be more vulnerable with more people than I had ever been.

I might never have found the courage to do it…if the apostle Paul hadn't led the way for me. That great missionary from Tarsus provided me with a wonderful model for what I planned to do. Here was a man whose life Jesus had radically changed. He had met Jesus face to face and had ministered for the Lord as he walked in the Spirit. He had witnessed great miracles: jail doors flinging open, chains falling off, conversions of the most unlikely people. If anyone could stand before others and present a picture of perfect faith and life, it was Paul. Yet rather than give us the impression he had it all together, this man provided a great example of vulnerability. He does it best in Romans 7.

It strikes me that we have allowed overfamiliarity to rob this passage of its astonishing power. I recommend that you read it in a different translation—perhaps *The Message* or *The New Living Translation*—to shake you loose from old, familiar moorings. In this amazing chapter, Paul admits that he does *not* have it all together. Jimmy Carter's admission to "lust in my heart" in the infamous 1976 magazine article is nothing compared to Paul's confessional. Within these verses, he admits to a fierce personal struggle raging within his members—a contest so powerful that the very thing he wants to do, he sometimes can't. What's more, the very things he knows he should not be doing, he sometimes does! This man who had been through so much for Christ, openly declares he is still imperfect and terribly prone to sin.

I find that both amazing and consistent with everything I read in Scripture. God did not edit out the imperfections of his people. David, a man after God's own heart, has his cowardly adulterous affair recorded in detail. Not only that, but the murder of his lover's husband is also right there in black and white. Whether it is David or the bigoted attitude of a reluctant prophet named Jonah, the imperfections of God's people are recorded throughout Scripture. Finally along comes Paul and writes what we all know to be true but find so difficult to admit: that we all struggle and sin, no matter how good we try to look. Paul set the example for me on the broadcast.

MAN ON THE SPOT

That first day, I took my place behind the microphone, accompanied by the best counselors in the Christian faith. They had Ph.D.'s; all I had was my struggles. During the first few months, I began to reveal who I was. As people thanked me over the air for sharing my problems, I became bolder. I let them know I had not done it right. I had known the truth and turned from it early in life, but I was grateful to have returned to God's way.

The response was amazing. People wanted more.

My colleagues, John Townsend and Henry Cloud, began to do the same. Although they are some of the wisest men I know, they refused to imply that wisdom brings perfection. They admitted they were far from perfect. As we focused on the truth of Scripture and revealed our own struggles (with humor rather than condescension), other stations began to add our program. The response to "reality Christianity" has been a great reward for us all. Consider an excerpt from a fax we received after one of our shows where I shared honestly about my life and marriage:

> I listen to your program every day. I sometimes tape the show,
> and luckily I taped the show on Monday. Good thing, or I
> might have thought I was imagining things. I started laughing
> and had to replay it a couple of times later, just to laugh again.

The reason I am so thankful to have taped it, though, is that we plan on playing it for our fifteen-year-old son and using it as an opportunity to teach him a little about healthy, Christian attitudes toward sexuality. Trying to live a moral life is tough enough without unnecessary condemnation.

I think Steve is one of the bravest people I know. When you boys share your vulnerabilities and failures, I am greatly encouraged. Through all of your books, videos, and radio shows, you guys have helped me more than you'll ever, ever know. I'm sure there are thousands or millions like me.

What a rewarding note—and all I did was reveal who I was! I took that risk because I know that being vulnerable leads to freedom. I know that when we protect ourselves with secrecy and hypocrisy, we build a prison inside ourselves that locks away our hearts from others. And I know that we fill up on pride when we refuse to be vulnerable.

I have made many mistakes, but one thing I have gotten right in recent years is seeking to be more open and vulnerable. I think that is why I am still married to Sandy after eighteen years. I think that is why I am not in the back ward of some mental hospital or walking the streets looking for a job. I believe secrecy would have destroyed me.

WHY IS IT SO HARD?

I have never known anyone to suffer more from being vulnerable than from being secretive about who they are. I've often said it would be better for our problems to be printed in the church bulletin and read by everyone on Sunday than for us to go to church without anyone knowing our struggles.

But if vulnerability is so good and so helpful, then why is it so hard for most of us to achieve? Why do so few of us risk it?

I think a lot of us resist opening up because we're afraid others will ostracize us when they discover we're not perfect or that our image doesn't match reality. Many times our fear of being rejected prevents us from connecting with people who may have shared the same kind of struggle we are facing. And somehow we don't see that by sharing we can give hope to fellow strugglers. So we protect ourselves and thus miss another opportunity to connect and to minister to people.

James 5:16 tells us, "Confess your sins to each other and pray for each other so that you may be healed." If we don't confess our sins to each other, how will we know how to pray for one another? By refusing to be vulnerable, we miss the chance not only to heal, but also to grow and to be strengthened. If we want to be healthy, we must overcome our pride and be willing to let people know how we're living and where we are, both spiritually and emotionally.

The church services I attend at Saddleback Community Church offer a great example of vulnerability. Almost every Sunday several individuals give testimonies in which they reveal what they went through before they came to Christ and what the Lord has done in their life since they received him. A few reveal current struggles. You can almost feel a sense of hope ripple across the congregation as these folks recount their spiritual journeys.

The fact is, none of the great revivals or spiritual renewals of history have occurred without open confession, without people willingly admitting not only that they had failed, but that they were turning their lives over to the Lord. Being vulnerable not only connects us to others, but it can also start a revival in a church or even a nation. To admit our sin, to be vulnerable, may even be the difference between spiritual greatness and holy catastrophe.

Contrast the lives of two ancient Israelite kings, Saul and David. While David is known in Scripture as the "apple of God's eye" and "a man after God's own heart," Saul is remembered chiefly for his rebellion and failure. Why the difference? Both men sinned in grievous ways. But when the prophet Nathan confronted David about his adultery, the shepherd king immediately admitted, "I have sinned against the LORD" (2 Samuel 12:13). When the prophet Samuel confronted Saul with his failure to carry out God's explicit instructions regarding the destruction of the Amalekite flocks, Saul answered, "The soldiers brought them from the Amalekites; they spared the best of the sheep and cattle to sacrifice to the LORD your God, but we totally destroyed the rest" (1 Samuel 15:15).

One king admitted, "I sinned—no one else." The other declared, "They sinned—not me." Could it be that vulnerability was the difference between the messianic future of one family line and the destruction of the other?

SECRECY KILLS

According to the Child Sexual Abuse Network, 80 percent of all molestation happens within religious homes. Why there? Because the perpetrators of this abuse cannot come out in their churches and say, "I need help." The people struggling in the vise grip of sexual compulsivity know they won't be embraced and patiently dealt with inside appropriate boundaries. So they stay hidden, anxiety-ridden and feeling like an alien in their own church and in their own bodies. Most will end up acting out their need for love and affection in totally inappropriate ways.

I [Jack] work in the area of sexual compulsivity. Many of my patients are pedophiles. I can't tell you how many men I've dealt with who struggle with this issue but cannot find the comfort and direction and healing of Jesus Christ in their own church because they can't admit anything. If they do, they know they'll be ostracized, even devoured. So the church community puts itself at risk because of its intolerance.

Tolerance, of course, doesn't mean accepting or enabling hurtful and sinful behavior; it simply means being willing to help the person within appropriate boundaries. Our moral judgment and condemnation of these strugglers keeps them from becoming vulnerable and admitting their problem.

Sam was a pedophile with sexual desire for young boys between the ages of five and eight. He came from a good Christian family and already knew what the Scripture said about his sin. It was a very bold step for him to come to someone like me. He knew that if he acted out, I would have to report him to the authorities. I assured him that if such a thing ever happened, I wouldn't abandon him but would walk with him through the restoration process. We emphasized that the problem was about his brokenness and not about a person so filled with sin that the devil "had" him.

Eventually Sam was able to start trusting me and grasping the concepts I provided. God allowed me to be a lamp unto his feet, to guide him out of this ugly behavior that he detested, to help him to find a way out of his darkness. He was ashamed of himself and felt convicted about his behavior, which told me God was working in his life. All he needed was for someone to be willing to be used by God to illuminate the path out.

But it didn't happen overnight! In fact, it took several years. Today Sam recognizes that when he feels tempted to act out, those feelings are an expression of his insecurity. At that moment he feels safer with a childlike love that sees him in an altruistic way than he does with people his own age. When he is able to frame the problem in this way, he can work with it. But as long as he sees his behavior as something damnable for which God is going to throw him into hell, he has to run from it and never face it.

Of course, it's difficult to hear somebody say, "When I rode by the school today, I saw this little boy who smiled at me, and I felt great temptation." It's difficult not to react to such a statement. It's difficult to access God's strength and realize that the speaker needs someone right then to provide a way out of his darkness, not someone to sit in judgment of him. It's *difficult*. But when someone risks being vulnerable with us—especially when the risk is so great—our Lord calls us to do the difficult thing. And he will give us the strength we need! Did he not say, "I tell you the truth, anyone who has faith in me will do what I have been doing. He will do even greater things than these, because I am going to the Father" (John 14:12)?

THE TRAP OF PERFECTIONISM

Many individuals who are unwilling to be vulnerable turn instead to perfectionism. These folks strive for perfection and make themselves sick in the process. Their priority shifts from believing in God to avoiding failure, ridicule, and criticism. They believe, irrationally, that if they can attain perfection, others will not be able to find fault with them or their actions. Only then, they believe, will they obtain the acceptance, love, and feeling of belonging they so desperately seek.

Followers of many unhealthy faith systems trap their victims into the tyranny of perfectionism. Because followers are taught they are members of an elite system, they believe they can and need to attain perfection—and they feel terrible shame when they fail.

These misguided folks are taught to believe that committing a sin means their faith is not strong enough. So they work harder to compensate for their supposed lack of faith. Perfectionists are driven by their desire to measure up to a standard that can never be attained. When they fail to reach that standard, they ratchet up their involvement in the toxic system in an attempt to measure up.

But it is confessing sin, not denying it, that frees people to learn and grow from their mistakes. Acceptance of the fact of our sinful human tendencies leads to the realization of our need for a divine Savior. In accepting Christ, Christians acknowledge that personal perfection can never be attained in this life. Healthy Christians want to avoid sin, but they are not so afraid of making a mistake that they are unable to experience the grace of God.

Perfectionism denies the right to embrace the limited nature of our human condition. It quickly becomes product-oriented; the person's relationship with God is considered less important than the product of "acceptable behavior." Anything short of perfection elicits the shame of not being good enough. Shame serves as the religious addict's "reward" for endeavoring to be Christlike and perfect.

Healthy faith, on the other hand, is not product-oriented but process-oriented. It balances texts like 2 Corinthians 13:11 ("Aim for perfection") with others like Psalm 119:96 ("To all perfection I see a limit"). Although we can never be perfect in this world, we can "aim for perfection" because we already have been accepted by God. Not measuring up does not bring shame; it brings about a change or repentance from sin. It validates our inability to be perfect and our need for a saving God.

Healthy faith accepts our full humanity and is rewarded with peace and serenity. In a healthy system where failure and mistakes are accepted as parts of the human condition, the process of growing closer to God and stronger in faith is valued. Fulfillment and satisfaction replace shame and remorse. Mistakes are accepted, along with the conviction that they will be corrected with the help of God.

In a healthy system, acceptance is based on love. Our Father, who is love, accepts us because of who he is and not because of what we do. Believers in a healthy system accept individuals because of who they are and not because of what they do or don't do. This acceptance frees individuals from the bonds of perfectionism and shame. And it allows them to be vulnerable and to quit pretending they can be perfect.

DO NOT FEAR

Repeatedly in Scripture we are told not to fear. "Do not fear...do not be afraid." Jesus himself said it often. In Matthew 10:26-28, for example, he said to his disciples about their opponents, "Do not be afraid of them. There is nothing concealed that will not be disclosed, or hidden that will not be made known. What I tell you in the dark, speak in the daylight; what is whispered in your ear, proclaim from the roofs. Do not be afraid of those who kill the body but cannot kill the soul."

Did you notice that the Master's remarkable call to courage is energized by his declaration of humankind's total vulnerability? Don't be afraid of anyone, he says, because no dirty little secret will remain hidden to harm you. All will be disclosed. All will be revealed. Everyone under heaven is vulnerable, so why not act like it when you have the choice?

If we believe the words of Christ, who tells us not to fear, we are free to be vulnerable. Being vulnerable means being *real.* It is the ability to risk rejection by laying before others all that we are and are not. If our faith is in God, we don't need to fear being real. The stronger our faith, the more we are driven to be real. Being accepted by God is much more important than being accepted by others. When we know God has accepted us, we can face rejection by others. As Isaiah asks us,

> Who are you that you fear mortal men,
> > the sons of men, who are but grass,
> that you forget the LORD your Maker,
> > who stretched out the heavens
> > and laid the foundations of the earth,
> that you live in constant terror every day
> > because of the wrath of the oppressor,
> > who is bent on destruction? (Isaiah 51:12-13)

And as the book of Proverbs reminds us, "Fear of man will prove to be a snare, but whoever trusts in the LORD is kept safe" (29:25).

Healthy faith frees us to come out of hiding and share our imperfect selves with others. Ephesians 6:16 tells us that we can use our faith as a shield. We don't have to conceal ourselves behind a facade. We can hold firm to our shield of faith and be vulnerable to others. A true test of faith is how much a person is willing to risk rejection by the world. The mark of the faithful is vulnerability with others.

DO YOU HAVE WORK TO DO?

Healthy Christians can admit their struggles, their failures, their sins, their emotional weaknesses. They do not have to pretend they are always on top of the world; they do not have to present a picture of continuous and perfect competency. They can admit when they are wrong, and they seek out help when they need it. In a word, they are *real.*

If your faith has you tied up and bound in secrets from your past, you have work to do. Seek out others who are willing to open up their lives to you. Use them and the example of the apostle Paul to confirm that real faith is a confessing and open faith.

With God in control, you have nothing to lose by being real—except your pride.

And that's a good thing.

CHAPTER 9

CUT ME SOME SLACK

A Healthy Faith Is Nondefensive and Nonjudgmental

There is only one Lawgiver and Judge, the one who is able to save and
destroy. But you—who are you to judge your neighbor?

James 4:12

Who's defensive? You certainly can't mean *me!*

Touchy? I am NOT! No way! You've got me all wrong.

Judgmental? How dare you! Why—you're nothing but a troublemaker!

Sometimes it isn't so easy to let down our defenses, is it? When it comes
to protecting a delicate ego, we are ever so reluctant to call off our personal
guard dogs and disarm our electric fences. In our sinful nature, most of us
are surrounded by more minefields than in Kosovo. If you try to gently lay a
little criticism within my defense perimeters, watch out! You may meet with
an explosion.

A friend of mine told me about walking right-of-way for a gas pipeline
company one summer when he was in college. In many ways, it was a great
job. Lots of sunshine and exercise, walking through the countryside over a
large pipeline buried fourteen feet below. There were, however, the inevitable
bulls, bees…and irascible farmers.

One day his journey took him through a certain farmer's field—an old man with something of a reputation with the gas company. The fact was, he didn't like *anybody* on his land, right-of-way or no. After testing an electric fence to make sure it was disarmed, the young gas worker prepared to step over the barrier. In a most vulnerable position, while he was straddling the wire, he saw out of the corner of his eye the farmer running for the barn. It didn't occur to my friend that the landowner was running for the power switch, but he was!

You and I may not have literal minefields or electric fences protecting our turf, but let's face it—each of us can be very sensitive at times. And more often than not, we are like that farmer running to the barn. The moment we see someone in a vulnerable position, rather than turn up the grace, we turn up the power and the heat—especially if their precarious situation makes us look better. We search for the weak and further enfeeble them with our quick judgments, and then we defend our own flaws as "at least not as bad as theirs." So we judge and defend ourselves into a rut of denial and thus offend those who are looking for a safe place to belong. We do this with our lives and we do it with our beliefs.

There is another way.

HEALTHY FAITH IS NONDEFENSIVE

Healthy faith takes a nondefensive position toward those who challenge its beliefs and exercise. In fact, healthy faith welcomes critical evaluation and tough questions as opportunities to learn and relate. Those with healthy faith refrain from constantly "defining" the truth for others and welcome the chance to share what they have tasted and experienced of the truth in their own lives. Those who question their faith are not automatically labeled and rejected as troublemakers. Instead, they are encouraged by those with a healthy faith to explore their doubts.

On the other hand, those in a toxic, unhealthy faith system are afraid of every perceived threat to that system. They feel personally threatened because much of their faith is dictated by their rules rather than by the Word of God. When God is in charge, there is no reason to feel threatened. He is in control, and he will champion the faith. He can handle any challenge!

When I was growing up, almost everyone I knew was a Christian (or at least tried to act like one). Disbelievers and doubters were unwelcome. And that went double for agnostics—that confused, accursed breed, full of doubt and disbelief.

So imagine my surprise when one day a friend of mine, a non-Christian, informed me that *I* was an agnostic! "You go to a Christian school," he told me, "but you're kind of an agnostic, aren't you?"

I was horrified. "What do you mean?" I stammered. "Why did you say that?"

"I just look at what you do," he replied. "You don't seem to spend time doing the things other Christians do, and you sure do a lot of things they would never do, so I just assumed that you were not too sure what you believed. That means you're an agnostic."

Now this was an incredibly observant person, so I couldn't write off his comments. Sure, I went to church, prayed, and read the Bible some, but I did not live out my faith. I would never have called myself an agnostic, but that's what I was.

If I had told anyone that I was an agnostic, they would have distanced themselves from me in a heartbeat. And here an unbeliever was confronting me with proof of my own unbelief! It was not easy to accept his conclusions, but God used them to help bring me back to him.

I wonder how much sooner I might have returned had I been allowed to admit what I was going through. I was a broken man, angry at God for not protecting me from my own bad decisions. I questioned whether he or his Word should mean anything to me. If I could have been open about my struggles, maybe I would not have wasted so much time. But because I had seen how doubters were treated in my church, I kept my faithlessness under wraps.

Years later I witnessed a completely different approach to agnosticism. I heard a minister actually congratulate the agnostics in his audience. "Are any of you here agnostics?" he asked. "You don't have to raise your hand if you are, but I want you to know that we love you and God loves you. And we respect you. You don't just buy into something because everyone else does. You want to make sure it is real. That you are agnostic shows you are searching, looking for truth, unlike the atheist who has decided there is no God. You want to find the real God, and I welcome your doubts and questions. I believe you will find the true God here at this church." Then he invited anyone full of doubt or disbelief to join him for a special time when together they could discuss any important matters of faith.

What a healthy, nonjudgmental approach to doubts and doubters! And because of that approach, many who never would have stepped forward with their doubts did so, enabling them to discover and accept truth and enter into a relationship with Jesus Christ.

Healthy faith is like that. It attracts people; it doesn't repel them. Those who become touchy and defensive repulse other people; they forget how incredibly attractive Christ was as he drew people to himself. What a relief to the healthy believer to not have to defend every criticism made by everyone outside the faith!

BEAR ONE ANOTHER'S BURDENS

In Galatians 6:2 we are instructed to bear one another's burdens. Rather than highlight a misstep of a fellow believer, we are to walk in his steps, hold onto him, and lead him to solid ground. Such a verse is easy to read but hard to implement—especially when the person who is faltering is a spouse.

Suppose a wife, distressed over a household situation, misjudges and mischaracterizes her husband's motives. A mature husband refuses to condemn his wife and is tolerant of her discomfort and disappointment. He is willing to be seen as the "bad guy" because he has made a decision not to go to war over her unfair assertions. No, he isn't happy about being characterized as "cheap" or "too greedy." Who would be? But he tolerates those unfair statements. He cares more about her state of being in that moment than protecting his own image.

Tolerance refuses to judge someone merely because he or she has judged you. When we act like that, the air in our home emits the fragrance of Christ.

Galatians isn't the only book where Paul calls us to bear each other's burdens; he does the same thing in several other letters. I think one of the greatest, most underrated verses in the Bible is the "little" command Paul slips into his letter to the believers at Colosse. He writes, "Bear with each other and forgive whatever grievances you may have against one another. Forgive as the Lord forgave you" (Colossians 3:13). Here he adds the need to forgive with the call to bear with one another. Put up with one another, he says. Hang in there with one another. Cut one another some slack. Tolerate one another, remembering that you, unworthy as you are, have been forgiven of all your sins by Jesus Christ.

Can you imagine how such a response could play out on the world scene? I'm reminded of a Palestinian gentleman I [Jack] know, whose family was displaced by the Israelis back in 1948. It has taken a long time and huge infusions of the grace of Christ, but this man has finally washed his hands of prejudice and hate. He has perspective enough (now) to see that the Jews, too, were a mistreated people, that they had been turned out of their homes and businesses in Germany and Eastern Europe. When they arrived in Palestine, they in turn displaced many of the people who had lived there for generations.

Over the years this man came to grasp the bigger issues. It isn't just Arab versus Jew, it is one more incident in the long history of man's inhumanity to man. This Palestinian gentleman is mature enough to admit that, in his own flesh, he is capable of committing some of the same acts—or worse. Only by the grace of God through the work of Jesus Christ in his life has he been able to let go of his prejudice and hatred.

Those who are caught up in unhealthy faith systems, however, are extremely intolerant of varying opinions or expressions of faith. You must either walk their way or you are out of step. Their rigidity rejects other believers and refuses to accept them. They routinely judge others and find the negative in everyone else's life. From a position of superiority, they put down others for what they believe and how they live out their faith. Those with an unhealthy faith want to control others, especially their beliefs.

One man, a member of a conservative group, lived in fear that his sons would veer into a more liberal faith or possibly end up with no faith at all. He believed that, in God's eyes, one of the most beautiful pictures is a family going to church together. He took his family to church twice every Sunday and also on Wednesday nights. If the church doors were open, he walked through them with his little tribe in tow.

His oldest son had some friends who attended another church on the edge of town. He liked it much better than his father's church. He asked to leave his parents' church to attend the other one. It was no strange religion or cult; in fact, it was part of the same denomination.

But that defensive father couldn't handle it. He forbade his son to attend the other church. He wanted the entire family to attend church together, and nothing would stand in the way of that goal. He was intolerant of his son's expressions of faith and of the other church and its members. His demands caused a severe split between him and his son. It was not their first problem, but it was the biggest. Tremendous bitterness and resentment grew from it and destroyed their ability to relate to each other.

Those with unhealthy faith routinely sacrifice relationships with family and friends to uphold some standard or ideal of their own. Believing that they are doing what God would have them do, they won't hesitate to push their ideas on others and judge them as less faithful and less in touch with the way things should be done. Certain they are upholding God's standards, they try to control others by demeaning their beliefs and practice of faith. They create a fake faith and a legalistic caricature of what faith is. Their children, resisting this intolerance, flee from their parents' faith and often never seek a relationship with God.

These parents succeed in winning a few battles, but at a terrible price!

HEALTHY FAITH IS NONJUDGMENTAL

Healthy believers don't judge what people say, but listen to what others have to offer. They evaluate it; they do not judge it. When we judge others, we accept them only conditionally. Healthy faith removes the conditions and the need to judge.

In the beautiful Sermon on the Mount, Christ gives us specific instructions about judging others. In Matthew 7:1 he instructs us not to judge others or we will be judged in the same way. All too often we are guilty of the very things we point out as wrong in others. Those with a growing, healthy faith stop judging people and start listening to them. When this occurs, compassion and empathy develop in their hearts.

Healthy believers look for similarities of experience that might help establish a relationship. Each person is seen as a fellow struggler in a different stage of the struggle. Healthy believers are so busy developing a personal relationship with God that they have no time to judge where others might be in their relationship.

Our ministry, New Life Treatment Centers, has had to fight its own battles with judgmental Christian spokesmen—almost from day one. We believe that solid Christians also need good, strong clinical training to be the best counselors ever. Others insist that anything tainted with psychology has to be wrong. They roundly condemn our approach because we use a secular discipline in our ministry.

Admittedly, there is a great deal wrong with modern psychology and where some of its practitioners have taken it. We need to be discerning and careful to determine what is good and helpful. From our point of view, psychology is simply a science that helps us to unearth problems and conflicts so that we might better minister. It is no threat to our faith, but a tool to help us deal with a fallen human nature that so often stands in the way of our relationship to God and others. I liken that to archaeology, also a science, that uses scientific techniques to unearth ancient artifacts that support and confirm the accuracy of the Bible. No, not everything is good about science, but we can use certain things from science to make our ministry stronger. Ultimately, all truth is God's truth, whatever label you put on it.

There are those, however, who are not content simply to reject our approach. For whatever reason, they seem to feel they must also attack, undermine, and if possible, destroy what we seek to do. Some large ministries have spoken out against us, attacking us in print or on radio or TV. I've personally called some of the folks involved in these attacks and said, "Let's get together and find out what your objections are, so that we're in this together. The enemy is not you or me; the enemy is a powerful supernatural being. If we spend our time arguing with each other, we'll never do anything to counter the enemy."

As a result of a few of these contacts, our ministry and some of those who opposed us gathered in Denver. I anticipated a big confrontation with those who railed against "the evils of psychology." On the way to the meeting, I noticed several members of a cult group sitting together, discussing what I presumed to be a strategy for drawing more and more vulnerable men, women, and teenagers into their mind-numbing system. I recognized the leader, a man who lectures around the world, teaches regularly on PBS, and usually has a couple of books on the bestseller list. Sadly, he has no idea who Jesus is or how he differs from other religious figures.

Suddenly I felt weary and a little depressed. Why did we have to waste our time and energy arguing and publicly debating with other Christian ministries while Satan's troops are on the march all over the world? I thought, *Here I am, on my way to argue with these Christian pastors. Instead we should be joining hands and sitting down and talking to these guys, trying to present Christ in a way they can accept. But because these ministries are so defensive of their territory and so judgmental of anybody who doesn't believe exactly the way they believe, we're wasting our energy and missing priceless opportunities to share the gospel all along the way.*

SLAPPING ON LABELS

Understand, there's a big difference between "judging" and "disagreeing." There is plenty of room for church people to disagree about the pros and cons of psychology. But slapping a label on someone's forehead is judgmental. I [Jack] was at a conference when *Toxic Faith* first came out. To this day, I remember a man waving a finger in my face and calling me a "psycho-heretic."

The purpose of labeling is to separate and divide. For example, in our society someone who has conservative beliefs is often labeled a "fundamentalist." The label no longer describes the approach by which that person evaluates life; it now describes the person. Someone who thinks that fundamentalist views are narrow focuses on the holder of those views and labels him narrow-minded. The focus moves from the person's views to the person's individuality. The person is shamed and demeaned for beliefs that have little to do with his value or his unique gifts from God. Disqualification by labeling is a poisonous practice all too characteristic of toxic faith.

Because it is difficult to rally against rational people who have distinctly different views, labels are used to polarize the opponents and energize the followers to fight. The enemy is disqualified so the underlying issues can be avoided. The possibility of finding the truth in the opposing argument is destroyed when labels are put in place. For example, calling someone narrow-minded may produce the desired effect. No one wants to follow a narrow-minded person or even be associated with one. A narrow-minded person is of no consequence, so that person is eliminated as a competent opponent.

Those with unhealthy, toxic faith find labeling a convenient activity; they use rumor and innuendo to kill the reputation of a sincere person who disagrees, for they know other people are more apt to agree with their position if a label has dehumanized the dissenter. A healthy person and a healthy faith, on the other hand, can disagree with the merits of another's system without making the judgment personal.

When he walked this earth, Jesus dealt with a number of groups, but his eyes always focused on individuals. He refused to label and reject people. Instead, he reached out to tax collectors, Samaritans, teachers of the law, prostitutes, the wealthy, and destitute beggars. Yes, he was harsh with teachers of the law and Pharisees; yet when Nicodemus came to him at night, he was gentle and lovingly received the man.

PIE IN THE SKY?

Even if I have to measure my progress in inches, I am determined to learn how to relate to people without being judgmental or defensive. If you work up the nerve to tell me about some shortcoming you notice in me, instead of immediately telling you the seventeen reasons why I do what I do, I am determined to take the time to hear you out. Instead of handing you your head on a platter, I want to choose to respond something like this: "Really? I guess I wasn't aware of that. Why don't you tell me about it? Is it something that disappoints you? Challenges you? What exactly am I doing that bothers you so?" And rather than justifying myself to the hilt, I will begin to explore that troublesome area with you.

Does that sound like pie in the sky? It's not. It's perfectly possible. By God's grace, we can do it. And don't you see how such an approach could stop an argument before it starts? How it might defuse a conflict before it ever blows up? A husband, for instance, who notices his wife has been hurt or upset, begins immediately to focus on that hurt, rather than launching into some protracted (and generally useless) justification for why he said what he said or did what he did.

Let's imagine a couple who needs to sell their house before buying the new one they really want. They get a firm offer, but in the husband's view, it is inadequate. He wants to reject the offer and hold out for a better deal. His wife, however, fears the loss of the house she really wants. Disappointment wells up in her throat and she snaps at her husband: "You know what I think? I think you're just being cheap. All *you* care about is money!"

Ah, the gauntlet has been tossed. Fort Sumter has just been fired upon. It's the ideal opportunity for a sharp argument that may quickly escalate into a small war, leaving husband and wife wounded for days to come. Satan rejoices at such situations, because as Paul tells us in Ephesians 4:26-27, the enemy gains a strong foothold in the lives of those who tolerate long-simmering anger and resentment.

But wait! This husband refuses to take the expected tack. He does not run for the barn to arm the electric fence. Instead of arguing or justifying his position, he replies, "Hon, if I had known this would bother you or hurt you like this, I would have been more than happy to close this deal. I care about you, not the house."

Wow! What spouse could keep an argument going with a response like that? It would be like trying to start a fire with wet wood. As Solomon taught us, a gentle answer turns away wrath (Proverbs 15:1). Instead of defending himself, this husband demonstrates genuine care and concern for his wife. In fact, he chooses to respond to her stress rather than to her hasty and ill-advised words (which she probably regretted as soon as they left her lips).

That, my friend, is a sign of a healthy, nondefensive faith. It's a faith that relaxes in its object and feels no necessity to retreat or counterattack in the face of criticism.

MY HEAD WILL NOT REFUSE IT

While healthy Christians judge sin in their own lives and strive to overcome sinful tendencies with God's help, they do not gleefully search out sin in the lives of others. Where necessary, they do confront it, but other people's sin is not a central focus of their lives—and they certainly never relish or enjoy it. They do not appoint themselves guardians of the souls of others, nor do they become antagonistic or defensive whenever someone points out an area of weakness in their own lives or ministries. They embody the truth of Psalm 141:5: "Let a righteous man strike me—it is a kindness; let him rebuke me— it is oil on my head. My head will not refuse it."

I can think of a number of individuals on the contemporary Christian scene who exemplify a nondefensive, nonjudgmental attitude…the sort of attitude that attracts those who are seeking the truth.

Dr. Robert Schuller is one. Schuller has a ministry to those who would never hear of Christ if he didn't take his approach. Both in public and in private, I have heard this godly man declare his uncompromising faith in Jesus Christ as the only way to find eternal life and salvation. But because he doesn't minister just like everyone else, many individuals reject and condemn him.

Closer to home, I think of my own father. By God's grace, he was able to maintain a nondefensive, nonjudgmental attitude even when those around him questioned the reality and sincerity of his faith. When my brother was diagnosed with AIDS, my father asked him to come back home and took him in. He did not need to defend himself to his friends about his homosexual son dying from AIDS. Nor did he judge my brother and heap shame on him at a time when he needed love and affection and acceptance and help. As a result, my brother's relationship with the Lord was restored before he died.

My father honored his Father by taking that approach, when as an old redneck from Texas, he might have found it much easier to stand on his judgmental heels and pronounce condemnation on a son who had strayed.

I'm sure it wasn't easy for my father to reach out to my brother as he did. It went against his background and his natural instincts. But he did reach out, consciously choosing to reject both defensiveness and judgmentalism. And because of that wise and healthy choice, both he and my brother now enjoy each other's company in heaven.

I wonder, who might you see there if you chose to follow my father's example?

KISSES, NOT HISSES

As I finish this chapter, I am reminded of a Special Olympics event held in Seattle, Washington, a few years back. I especially remember the 100-yard dash, where nine mentally and physically challenged children competed against each other.

With great anticipation the runners lined up and waited for the gun. They were smiling and full of energy, hoping to win but thrilled just to compete.

The starting gun fired and all nine kids ran down the track as fast as they could. Suddenly one of the boys stumbled and rolled over. A gasp spread through the stands. Then, with no prompting, a little girl with Down's syndrome stopped, turned around, and went to the fallen boy. She knelt beside him and said, "Here, this will make it feel all better." Then she kissed him on the cheek.

One by one, the other special runners stopped and returned to the spot where the boy lay crumpled. They reached down and helped him up. Then, arm in arm, all nine of those wonderful kids went toward the finish together. They all crossed the line at the same time, so that all nine could win.

Rivers of tears flowed down the faces of the onlookers, who stood to their feet to applaud grace delivered when least expected.

Friend, we are all strugglers together, stumbling toward the finish line. We need each other. We need outstretched arms and kisses, not pointing fingers and hisses. It really is the only way to victory.

CHAPTER 10

HANDLE WITH CARE

A Healthy Faith Is Respectful of Others

Do nothing out of selfish ambition or vain conceit, but in humility consider others better than yourselves.

Philippians 2:3

Wherever the gospel of Jesus Christ has taken root and the Word of God has been taught and honored, respect for men and women has grown along with it. As healthy faith grows, mutual respect grows too. Where such respect is lacking or absent, either Scripture is not being taught or the gospel itself is being denied.

In 1 Timothy, we catch a glimpse of how respect bubbles up from the heart of a believer and flows into the tributaries of every relationship. Paul writes: "Do not rebuke an older man harshly, but exhort him as if he were your father. Treat younger men as brothers, older women as mothers, and younger women as sisters, with absolute purity. Give proper recognition to those widows who are really in need" (5:1-3).

Seniors. Older men. Older women. Younger men. Younger women. Singles. Widows. Children. The needy. Historically, these groups have not always known and experienced the respect and honor of the community. Yet Paul makes respect a priority—and the Holy Spirit makes sure his instruction gets embedded within the text of Holy Scripture to be with us forever.

Some time ago, I read about the work of a Wycliffe Bible translator in a remote village in Papua New Guinea. When the opening chapters of Genesis were first translated into the native language, the attitude toward women in the tribe changed overnight. They had not realized or understood that the woman had been specially formed out of the side of the man. Without even hearing this concept developed, these people immediately grasped the idea of equality between the sexes and began adjusting their behavior. The people heard. They believed. They obeyed. They changed. Just like that.

That change doesn't mean everyone in the tribe immediately came to faith in Christ, however. While they immediately recognized the respect God has for both men and women, the members of this tribe had their own hard-to-abandon gods and superstitions. One of their practices was to spit on the wounds of the sick. Their medicine men were known as the spitters, and they did not want someone like Jesus to take away their status in the village.

However, that attitude changed as more of the Bible was translated into the tribe's dialect. When translators read the passage where Jesus cured a blind man in a most unusual way, the medicine men pricked up their ears. The Master spit on the ground, made a paste of mud, put it on the man's eyelids, told him to wash it off—and the man was healed. When these tribesmen heard this story in their own language, they saw that Jesus was not against them, but for them. They found one of their own, a Savior who was also a spitter! And they came to the Lord because of this connection.

I can't help but wonder if, a couple of thousand of years ago, Jesus used this unusual method of healing just for these medicine men of Papua New Guinea? I wonder if he respected their uniqueness so much that long ago he laid the foundation for them to be won to God? It wouldn't surprise me. After all, when Jesus was asked to name the greatest commandment, he cited—as many of his listeners anticipated and expected that he would—" 'Love the

Lord your God with all your heart and with all your soul and with all your mind.' This is the first and greatest commandment" (Matthew 22:37-38).

Fine. No problem. Approving nods all around. But Jesus refused to stop there. He then added, "And the second is like it: 'Love your neighbor as yourself.' All the Law and the Prophets hang on these two commandments" (verses 39-40).

To a group of self-satisfied, self-justifying Pharisees, Jesus took the familiar teaching about wholehearted love for God and linked it with love and respect for others. This other-focused living is a hallmark of authentic, healthy faith.

NO NEED TO FEEL THREATENED

When our security depends on God, we can appreciate people for their strengths *and* their weaknesses. Differing views and perspectives can be seen as a result of different people at different places in the progression of a growing faith. When a healthy faith sets the agenda, those who are of different denominations or even from different factions within a denomination are no longer perceived as the enemy.

Throughout the Bible, God instructs us to cultivate respect for all people. He warns against showing favor to any one group, such as the wealthy. James rolls up his sleeves and delivers a body blow to the church when he writes: "Have you not discriminated among yourselves and become judges with evil thoughts?" (James 2:4).

We need to see each person as a wonderful creation of God with gifts and talents sent directly from God. Faith frees us from the fear of others and allows us to love them. If we have healthy faith, we can love our brothers and sisters and trust God to work on their problems as we pray for him to do so. First Peter 2:17 tells us to show proper respect for everyone and to love all believers. When faith grows to this level of respect and acceptance of others, it frees us to serve God. What a contrast to unhealthy or toxic faith systems! Too often those enmeshed in such organizations attack, attack, attack others out of their own insecurities.

WE HAVE MET THE ENEMY AND—HE ISN'T!

A great example of growing, mutual respect among believers has been the amazing Promise Keepers movement of the past decade. Pastors of different denominations and traditions have found themselves grasping hands and praising God with those they formerly regarded as the competition—if not the enemy. Many once trapped by longstanding habits of judgmentalism and bickering over nonessential issues have caught a wider vision. They have stood shoulder to shoulder with tens of thousands of brothers, singing "How Great Thou Art," and have been moved to the core of their being.

Worship has leveled the playing field.

Worship has placed the focus back on Jesus Christ.

A strong emphasis at Promise Keepers has been love and respect between different races and cultures. As a result of much effort and fervent prayer, black and white and Asian and Native American leaders have publicly embraced, declaring their love for one another in Christ. Old suspicions and prejudices have been laid at the foot of the cross…where they belong.

Two thousand years ago the apostle Paul showed us this was possible. While he was imprisoned in Rome, Paul had good reasons for questioning the motives of some who were preaching in the name of Jesus. He had a strong impression that their pro-Jesus message was weighted with an anti-Paul bias. Imprisoned as he was for boldly declaring the gospel, that could have been a tough pill to choke down.

But in one of those great about-faces so characteristic of Paul, he suddenly said, in effect, "You know what? I don't give a rip what their motives are. Because every time they get up to preach, the name of Jesus is being proclaimed. That's what life's all about! And I'm going to be happy about that and applaud, instead of working myself into a dither or throwing apostolic tomatoes." (See Philippians 1:15-18.)

We all need a healthy dose of that attitude. When Jesus is proclaimed, we need to cheer—even if we don't like the way the guy talks or agree with all the fine points of his presentation. Many of us disagree, for instance, over the mode of baptism. I have my own opinions on the subject, and I think I could do a fair job giving you biblical reasons for them. But what would I gain? With time slipping away and eternity looming before us, what does it matter whether you are dunked, sprinkled, poured on, or doused with a fire hose? Rather than focusing on techniques to the point that we divide the body of Christ over them, we ought to be asking, "Do these people really believe in Jesus? Have they truly appropriated his saving grace? Do they understand who he is and why he came?"

If we can agree on those issues, if we can join hands on those priorities, then we can overlook a lot of less important details regarding traditions, histories, cultural differences, and on and on. And on and on some more. We can respect one another because we are all children of God, chosen by him from before the foundation of the world and equipped with unique ministries for the health of the greater body.

Respecting another person is simply admitting that God is big enough to love him or her just as much as he loves me.

SISTER ACT

Recently our organization held a Women of Faith conference in a large, predominantly Catholic, Texas city. A number of the nuns in this city became intrigued by our content but weren't sure whether our program was something they could endorse.

So what did they do? Fire missiles at us? Issue warnings to the faithful? Encourage a boycott? Dismiss us out of hand?

No! None of the above. They decided to give us a try. And before the first evening was over, these wonderful nuns were laughing, clapping, listening, and thoroughly enjoying themselves. Soon they found themselves clasping hands and hugging people of other denominations whom they never would have met if they hadn't taken the risk of attending our conference. During that event, they cultivated a wider respect for other people of faith who live in their city.

Sadly, I have quite a bit of firsthand knowledge about disrespecting people. Somehow, I grew up with a destructive message about women. Early in my life, I saw women as objects to be used and discarded at will. When I had a girlfriend, I almost thought of myself as *wearing* her, rather than being with her. The way I saw it, the girl was there to complement me and to serve me. To make matters worse, I picked up some of these unhealthy, unbiblical attitudes toward women in church! I came to see women as placed on this earth only to serve men. Suffice it to say, I had little respect for the feminine gender.

As you might imagine, this attitude didn't fly very far in marriage. When those selfish and disrespectful ideas about women crashed into the daily reality of matrimony, my first marriage exploded into a pile of splinters. There I was in seminary, studying to become the world's greatest Christian marriage counselor—and my wife divorced me! Not exactly a good foundation for my chosen career. I left school and went a different direction with my life. With no friends and no future, I felt I had no place in God's kingdom. It took a long time for the pain to diminish to a tolerable level.

You would think a guy would learn a few things from a trauma like that. And I really thought I had. But I was wrong. In my second marriage (which has now lasted eighteen years), I can still remember the day Sandy said to me, "How would you feel about living somewhere else?"

"Somewhere else?" I replied. "But—we love it here! I don't see any reason for us to move. Where did this come from?"

"I didn't say *us*," she replied. "I said *you*. How about *you* living somewhere else?" At that point I realized how little I had grown in my attitudes about women. I quickly went into counseling, and with God's help (and Sandy's long-suffering patience), I began to seriously address those issues. Through the Lord's faithfulness, I changed the way I viewed women and began to respect them. In fact, one of the great joys of my life today is to work with the women God has placed in my life. These days, I have contact with some incredible women who are not only fine executives and gifted managers, but also great people of faith.

Do you want to hear something ironic? Since those humbling days of self-revelation, the Lord has given me a vision for women's conferences, where the underlying theme is a respect for women that encourages them to develop their relationship with the Lord. We call these conferences "Women of Faith," and we reach hundreds of thousands of women each year. In our teaching we urge women to be free of the bondage others try to put on them through false teaching. Those conferences offer no specific agenda of God's will for each woman; instead, we challenge women to discover for themselves God's will for their lives. Presenting God's truth with grace is our mission.

In addition to the conference ministry, I have a radio program with an audience composed mainly of women. Best of all, I have a wife and a daughter who love me. My goal is to serve all these women in a greater way than ever before.

NO PUT-DOWNS!

The problem I struggled with earlier in my life wasn't unique to me. At one of the Women of Faith conferences a woman came up to several of us and said, "I have enjoyed this more than anything I've ever been a part of. I've been here through the whole conference, and no one has put me down." She was serious! That's what I call a bittersweet compliment. How sad that a major virtue of a Christian conference would be the fact that no one is disparaged! But the fact is, church leaders and teachers who mishandle the Scriptures do snub women.

One of the messages that Sheila Walsh gives at the Women of Faith conferences is "God has seen your movie, and he loves it." She's trying to communicate that a woman is not a second-class citizen in the eyes of God.

Sadly, many men who claim to be Christians use Scripture as a rationale for treating women as second-class citizens. The men demand their way in everything because "women need to submit." They force themselves on their wives and cruelly subject them to the worst of treatment—all in the name of "God's role for a woman." Any and all respect for a woman is lost in this unbiblical take on submission.

Yet in the very Ephesians 5 passage that some men are so fond of quoting, an even more profound teaching clamors to be heard: men are told to love their wives as Christ loved the church—to be willing to die for a woman as Christ died for the church. "Men," Paul says, "love your wives as you love your own bodies" (verse 28). These strong commands demand that a man respect his wife.

Any man who truly loves Christ will focus more on his need to sacrifice for his wife than on her need to submit to him. Then any woman who would not submit to such a man would be foolish. Under Christ's plan for husbands and wives, both individuals respect each other and love each other with the attitude of Christ.

Everywhere Christ takes control of a heart, respect for others is a necessary result.

A SINGLE PRIORITY

Women, of course, aren't the only ones who often suffer from a lack of respect. Did you know that sixteen million American children under the age of eighteen live with only one parent? In 87 percent of those cases, that one parent is a woman. In spite of that astounding statistic, many evangelical churches have no specific ministries aimed toward single parents. They may have a "singles ministry," but no specific encouragement and help for single parents.

Why? Oftentimes it stems from the belief that being single was the result of sin and divorce—and churches don't want to be seen condoning sin and divorce. So these struggling, hard-working, needy people are too frequently overlooked.

I can never forget what happened after my own divorce. The young married couples class met on the second floor of the church in a huge room, full of life and love and leadership. After my divorce, I left that class to join the other divorcees, who met in the basement next to the boiler room. I felt my back hunching over as I descended the stairs. When I entered the room, I felt humiliation and disgrace seeping from the pores of my fellow rejects. In dull silence we attempted to study God's message of grace—but we could not find it in the fog of Christian condescension.

That miserable time helped me understand that toxic churches operate under five basic rules grounded in false expectations and teachings:

1. If you are a real Christian, you will not have major problems like divorce.
2. If you do develop a major problem, it is the result of your deep spiritual weakness.
3. Since this weakness makes the church look bad, the least you can do is pretend you do not have this problem.
4. If you are not going to pretend you are problem-free, at least show everyone you are deeply ashamed.
5. If you are not going to either pretend to be perfect or act ashamed, don't show up.

So I stopped showing up.

What a wasted opportunity! I believe that if churches would boldly step into the lives of this modern-day equivalent of the Bible's "widows and orphans," they would find a field "white unto harvest." I firmly believe that if Jesus were here today, he'd be with those single moms and those struggling with the deep hurts of divorce, encouraging their hearts and ministering to their needs.

By ignoring these folks and failing to minister to them, we are showing a lack of basic respect. I frankly don't think many people would claim the church is "condoning sinful behavior" or "advocating divorce" just because we're ministering to men and women in painful life situations.

Feeling the terrible loneliness and isolation of their situation, many of these people remarry too soon. Once remarried, they reason, they'll have a place within the fellowship of God's people once more. Yet the truth is that we need to be encouraging these men and women to come to a place where they can say, "God, whether or not I ever marry again, you are the most important person in my life. You are my priority. I want to grow in you. I want to send my roots down into your love. If I don't marry, I will be a great parent by your grace and with your help. If I do marry, I will be a great parent and a loving spouse. But in all of that, I will be committed to you."

The opportunities to touch lives for Jesus Christ are great…if we will truly respect people.

THE UNTOUCHABLES

Okay, ministering to divorced men and women and to singles and children and respecting them is one issue. But what about homosexuals? I believe the gospel demands that we also respect homosexuals. Now—before I lose you— just what does respect look like in this situation? Do we respect that they're engaged in a sin that is an unnatural act, one that God abhors? No. But if we're ever going to win someone involved in homosexual behavior to the Lord, we must understand that this situation evolved out of real needs. No one just makes up these needs; they come from somewhere. The root problem may have been a smothering or overly domineering mother, an absent or passive father, exposure to pornography, or some early abuse or molestation.

Men and women turn down the sinful path of homosexuality for many reasons, but if we don't respect them as human beings, understanding that they possess real needs, then we will fail in our ministry to them. We may as well join those who stand outside of a homosexual's funeral, holding up signs that say, "God hates fags." (This is exactly what some misguided men and women did at the funeral of Matthew Shepard, the young man murdered in Laramie, Wyoming, in October 1998, largely because of his homosexuality). And if we can't do better than *that,* then we need to question whether we really understand who Jesus was and is.

Sometimes I wonder if people ever read the New Testament to see the way Jesus reached out to the "least of these" and touched and changed their lives. He had a way of walking right into the midst of untouchables. He had a way of shocking people by associating with outsiders and undesirables.

And he still would...if we will be his hands and feet, his heart and his voice.

THE FEAR IS GONE

I began our organization, New Life Clinics, back in 1988, after some individuals trusted me with two million dollars in start-up funds. I was scared to death. I had a degree in elementary education, a dual master's degree in counseling and administration, a big chunk of money—but only one year of business school. I was terrified by the prospect of failure and embarrassment and petrified of wasting the money of those who had placed their trust in me.

As a result, I sought to instill my terror throughout the organization. I cultivated the image of an intimidator and a tough boss. People may have respected my skills and abilities, but my rule-through-fear management style wasn't much fun to be around. If the truth were known, our organization was an unhealthy, demoralizing place to work.

Over the next few years, I watched this dysfunctional environment manifest itself among our people. Several had affairs. There were incidents of unethical behavior. Stupid decisions were made based on fear. The organization was a mess. Something had to change.

I had to change.

With all the pressure and stress and growth of the organization—and we did accomplish some great things—I had lost track of who I was. The desire for success had overtaken my desire for ministry and pleasing God. I was a people person who had morphed into a short-fused, fear-driven tyrant. Again, as in my marriage, I had to get down very low before the Lord to seek his forgiveness and then ask for the forgiveness of many others. I had to revisit the truth of 1 Peter 5:5: "God opposes the proud but gives grace to the humble." I had to humble myself under God's mighty hand, learning to respect my fellow employees as I desired to be respected.

Nobody changes overnight, but I have been encouraged by what the Lord has accomplished in my life. Not long ago, one of our long-term employees came to me and said, "I just want you to know that I have seen the change in you. I have the impression that God has bestowed upon you a renewed gift of love—and that the fear is gone." She then said, "I hope that everybody throughout the organization knows that managing with fear is the old style—and that it's been gone for a long time. If they're still emulating that old style, I hope they come to realize they're not growing along with you."

I was so thankful for those words! Thankful that, number one, the change had truly occurred; number two, that someone had noticed it; and number three, that it was making an impact on the organization.

I'm grateful God preserved the organization while he transformed me into a manager who respects people, who no longer uses my position of authority to inflict my agenda on others. In the process, I've developed a new respect for those we serve and a new regard for those who work with me. As an organization, we have gone from a problem-plagued company on the edge of bankruptcy to a ministry where you can sense God's Spirit in the hallways. I praise him for showing me that the error was not the error of others, but the error of a leader who refused to respect his people.

The result is that I also respect myself. And I have earned the respect of my wife, who is not easily impressed. The other day she said to me that she often talks to her friends about the change she's seen in me. That's the kind of comment that ranks right up there with the one my daughter gave me some time ago. "Daddy," she said, "you're as handsome as sweet-smelling perfume."

I'll take the compliment—but you and I both know where that perfume came from, don't we?

CHAPTER 11

STRONG CONNECTIONS

A Healthy Faith Is Relationship-Oriented

Let us consider how we may spur one another on toward love and good
deeds. Let us not give up meeting together, as some are in the habit of
doing, but let us encourage one another.

Hebrews 10:24-25

Years ago I read about some kids who built a clubhouse in the branches of a
tree. Wise beyond their years, these boys and girls came up with a few simple
rules for how to behave in this lofty little shelter. Scrawled out in childish
handwriting, three rules were posted outside the door:

NOBODY ACT BIG.

NOBODY ACT SMALL.

EVERYBODY ACT MEDIUM.[1]

That isn't bad counsel for relating to one another as believers. We are neither angels nor worms. We are all forgiven, redeemed sinners adopted into
the very family of God. We are all in the process of becoming more like our
Lord and on our way to eternal life in heaven. Together!

ESCAPING THE PERFORMANCE TRAP

"Together" is a key word in the Christian life. The New Testament makes it plain that relationships belong center stage in the church. That means that healthy faith is relationship-centered, not activity-focused or task-oriented. It values the individual for who he or she is as a son or daughter of God, not primarily for what he or she can do or contribute. Godliness depends on a growing walk with a personal God, not on adhering to a certain code of conduct laid down by the leader. Healthy faith bears in mind the apostle's instruction: "We know that we have passed from death to life, because we love our brothers. Anyone who does not love remains in death" (1 John 3:14).

God has shown us that the more we love him, the more we will seek out others and manifest his love in our relationships. Instead of being obedient to man-made rules, the person of healthy faith strives to develop intimacy with others. Sharing the faith and loving another in faith build one's relationship with God.

In unhealthy faith, the focus shifts from relationships to rules. The individual abandons most relationships, believing that God is all that matters. Once I discussed this problem with a minister. He told me that three years earlier he had been obsessed with himself and his own knowledge of God. The more his addiction grew, the more isolated he became from others. He had no time for people. He was short-spoken and most people loathed being around him. One day a woman who had supported the church for some time came to see him. She said she wanted to say only two words: "Forget yourself."

He asked her what she meant, but she said no more. He thought and thought about her statement. He became obsessed with learning what she meant. He called her and she told him she was coming for another visit the following week; she would give him two more words at that time. When she arrived, she looked him in the eye and said, "Serve others."

The woman's words revolutionized this minister's faith. He realized he had been serving himself and had forgotten the importance of relationships. He began to rebuild what he had torn down, and in so doing, his faith began to flourish.

Performance-driven believers focus on what they do in the name of God and what they perceive as the instant rewards sent from him, rather than placing their trust in God. In this way they come to totally rely on their own abilities to find divine favor. Their performance becomes everything, and they surround themselves with people willing to describe their performance as outstanding. Performance validates such an individual's worth and being, but every day becomes a new battle to regain their sense of self-worth.

Sadly, these unfortunate folk rarely feel good about their performance; they need waves of adulation to compensate for sagging egos. They live with the constant fear that whatever they do won't be enough, and they won't be able to pick up the pieces this time. If things are going well, they fear the other shoe will soon drop, and their fear leads to harder work and more effort.

The performance-oriented believer appears to be satisfied with his drive to achieve. Deep inside, however, he or she is desperately unhappy with the role, resents it greatly, and is ferociously angry about having to do so much and receive so little recognition for all the effort. So this individual lives with anger, unable to express it to anyone (except in violent outbursts) because he or she has no intimate friends with whom to share.

The New Testament blows away all of these performance standards, just as a sweet wind from the sea dissipates toxic fumes. Jesus consistently rejected such standards in those he called to his side. In Matthew 18 we are told: "He called a little child and had him stand among them. And he said: 'I tell you the truth, unless you change and become like little children, you will never enter the kingdom of heaven. Therefore, whoever humbles himself like this child is the greatest in the kingdom of heaven'" (verses 2-4).

What can a little child do except run into the open arms of God? What can a little boy or girl do but accept God's grace, love, strength, and help with a wide open heart?

Nothing more than that. And there is nothing more that God requires.

A Relational Mirror

In a healthy church, relationships flourish and grow as people focus on the number-one relationship with God. I don't think you can build an authentic relationship with someone else unless you first build one with God. The sweet overflow of that divine friendship leads to love for one another. As the apostle John put it: "If we walk in the light, as he is in the light, *we have fellowship with one another,* and the blood of Jesus, his Son, purifies us from all sin" (1 John 1:7). The way we relate to others often mirrors the way we relate to God.

The Pharisees, for instance, put on a great display of outward holiness. They wanted everyone to think they were intimate with God, wrapped in the mantle of his approval. Inside, however, they had lost their love for him. That fact showed most plainly in the way they treated others: They didn't care one bit that people's lives were weighted down by rules and legalism. Their attitudes were revealed clearly in statements like the one made to Nicodemus: "This mob that knows nothing of the law—there is a curse on them" (John 7:49).

If we really love the Lord, we will cultivate an inner, personal walk with him. We will spend time with him every day. We're going to experience him daily in Bible study and prayer and worship. And if we can't make that a priority, we're probably not making other relationships in our lives a priority either.

No Lone Ranger Christianity

Many people insist their faith and their walk with God are private, that they don't need to discuss them with anyone. But while our relationship with Jesus may be intimate and deeply personal, it is anything but a private affair! Throughout the New Testament, I see Scripture driving us to open relationships. The New Testament knows nothing of Lone Ranger Christianity.

James clearly instructs us to "confess your sins to each other and pray for each other so that you may be healed" (James 5:16). Confession is a bridge, something that strengthens a relationship and unlocks the chambers of shame that darken a person's soul, so he or she can experience a greater measure of freedom in Christ. Confession to Christ rips down the wall of guilt that rises each time we act irresponsibly. It also tears down the wall of guilt between us and other believers. Our pride widens that wall, but when we humbly confess to each other, it tumbles down so that intimacy can be restored.

Romans 10:9 speaks of another kind of confession: confessing with your mouth that Jesus is Lord. New Testament faith isn't some private meditation hovering in the back of the mind. It is a happy certainty—a reality to be spoken in the presence of listening ears.

Jesus gathered twelve disciples around him, "that they might be with him and that he might send them out" (Mark 3:14). Being with Jesus was just as important as preaching and casting out demons. And so it is with us. Living together and working side by side in relationship is one of the most Christ-exalting things we can do.

If you think you were called by God to be a Lone Ranger Christian, you're really dead in the saddle. So do you have a Tonto in your life? If not, find one and make that person your trusted companion.

RELATIONSHIP-ORIENTED CHURCHES

If I love someone, I will demonstrate that love through tangible acts. Likewise, healthy churches show genuine care and concern for each believer; toxic churches care for and are concerned about "The Program." In a healthy church, people always take priority over the program.

In a healthy church, the whole person is cared for and attended to—not the intellect alone, not the emotions alone. People talk to one another honestly about where they are on their spiritual journey and where they long to be. People are free to admit the sins and stumbling blocks in their lives with no sense of being a disappointment to some slick, whitewashed image the church wishes to project. They recognize that churches are spiritual hospitals where people are free to heal at their own pace under the care of the Great Physician. You should never be surprised to find sick or wounded people in a hospital! The very reason they've "checked in" is so that they might get better and become whole.

A healthy church lives by five rules quite different from the toxic laws mentioned earlier. These rules are based on truth and reality and connect us with other believers and fellow strugglers. Here they are:

1. Even as a Christian, you are going to have some major problems—but God will use these problems to grow your character. When you became a Christian, you did not instantly develop Christlike character. That takes time and effort, so expect a lot of struggle.

2. When hardship and heartache enter your life, don't make any rash conclusions about yourself or God. While your circumstances could be the result of some sin in your life, remember that everyone has sin in his or her life. Your trouble is quite likely the result of living in a fallen world where bad things really do happen to some very good people.

3. When you have a problem, don't pretend that you don't. The worst thing you can do is pretend. Healthy Christians want to meet your needs, but if you pretend, how will they know you have any? You will only grow increasingly fake. When no one pretends, we can all face reality together.

4. Don't place unneeded shame on yourself; it is too big a burden for you to carry around. God knows the nature of your sins, and all of us

have committed some big ones. The only legitimate reason for feeling shame is if you have not fully accepted the grace God has provided for you.

5. If you have to pretend, or if you feel great shame over some big problem, at least show up. Come as you are, broken or bruised. Just come! Be here with us, and we will struggle through this together.

Healthy churches also share another unspoken practice, one that you may miss since they don't advertise it. Their members are so committed to reaching out to hurting people that if you are in too much trouble to show up, if you are too ashamed to come, the people of a healthy church will come to you. They will find you and reach you and help you, whether you are in jail or somewhere else. This practice sets them apart from others, and it indicates that these believers are committed to loving you, even when it is hard.

My wife's faith is the kind you find in a healthy church. When one of our friends ended up in a shelter with her son, Sandy went there, met with her, and then brought them home to live with us for a couple of years. Those were sweet times we will never forget! And while I struggled with whether we would be safe in the presence of someone with AIDS, Sandy invited my brother to come and live with us. Because of her faith, he knew there was real love for him beyond what my mother and father provided. Her faith reflected the heart of her heavenly Father. We need more people like Sandy in churches all around the world, men and women who are committed to relational ministry even when it is not convenient or pretty.

Now don't make the mistake of thinking that participating in close relational fellowships is about big church versus small church! Most large churches today have scores of dynamic, small group fellowships within the larger congregation. This is such a healthy phenomenon that the bigger the church grows, the smaller it may actually feel, because more and more people are connecting in authentic relationships.

For any relationship to be authentic, of course, there must be love. Throughout my ministry, I have found many sick churches where love has withered and died. People sense they're being used or abused rather than loved, that there's no relationship-building between the minister and the congregation. But healthy churches demonstrate a growing sense of—and active concern for—people's relationship needs. We all live in a construction zone, and we all need one another.

THE VALUE OF ACCOUNTABILITY

A key aspect of maintaining healthy relationships is accountability; that is, the eager willingness to lay open your life to the caring gaze of another, revealing where you need to work and having the person regularly ask if you're doing that work. That's what real accountability is all about. It's saying, "I don't have the power within myself to live this life, and I don't care who knows it! I need to stay connected with God, and I need to stay connected with others who will help me continue growing in him."

Accountability not only helps us stay morally correct, but it also helps us to stay theologically correct. In the book of Acts, it was the Bereans who were called "noble of character" because "they received the message with great eagerness and examined the Scriptures every day to see if what Paul said was true" (Acts 17:11). When we submit to people who know the truth (and we're not out there trying to make it up on our own), we are much less likely to get into theological binds void of the truth of Jesus.

You've heard that love covers a multitude of sins? Indeed it does! And so does accountability! If God's people were in healthy, accountable relationships with others, toxic faith would never be allowed to flourish! Hear me, please: Anyone who claims to be so tied into God that he or she does not need to be tied into people is guaranteed to fail in faith and fail in ministering to the needs of people. God never intended anyone to be so focused on him that there is no need to stay connected with people. No one has a faith that can be free from accountability to others.

LEADERS ESPECIALLY NEED ACCOUNTABILITY

While accountability is important for everyone, it is critical for leadership. Unhealthy faith is often based upon the unchecked, unchallenged exercise of power. Healthy faith is based on personal relationship and on trust. As a leader, am I willing to take the advice of others? Am I willing to stand corrected? Am I willing to open my dealings to the light of day? Do I refuse to use my position as some kind of "holy club" to beat down the opinions and objections of others? Do I refuse to drop God's name into conversations or use Scripture to intimidate others so I can get my way?

Lack of accountability in any leadership structure is a clear warning that ought to flash before our eyes "DANGER! DANGER!" in red neon letters. It also indicates a lack of faith in God and the presence of a faith built on self-assertion and ego.

For this reason, when unhealthy faith practices come under scrutiny, its leaders react predictably. "I am accountable only to God!" they bellow. Listen—*no one* is accountable only to God! We are all accountable to the government. A married person is accountable to a spouse. Anyone asserting accountability only to God either is not thinking clearly or has a terrible sin to hide. When a leader makes such an assertion, people should clear out. A person accountable only to God is a person out of control. Such a person defines God in his or her terms, creates a religion around his or her needs, and then remains accountable to a false god created in his or her image.

The followers of a toxic faith leader who is not subject to accountability tend to avoid accountability also. They become little generals in a toxic army that, they claim, no one outside the organization understands. This stance cuts off all who would question their beliefs and practices and arms them with the right to do as they please. These little generals follow orders from their leader, believing they are on a mission from God, and refuse to listen to any input from others. Such a lack of accountability makes it difficult for members to turn away from the organization and back to a true faith in God. The result? Most continue in the unhealthy system and many eventually lose all belief in God. Without accountability, leadership goes to seed. The man with the unyielding hand on the steering wheel may drive the church—or a whole denomination—into the ditch.

I am haunted by some statistics I encountered recently. Seventy percent of United Methodists agree with the statement, "The Bible is God's Word and all it says is true." At the same time, however, 42 percent believe that "all religions are equally true." And among Lutherans, 67 percent say that they agree or probably agree with the statement, "Although there are many religions in the world, most of them lead to the same God."

When I see such statistics, I have to ask myself, "What has happened to the leadership in these groups?" Those in authority have become unaccountable, detached, and tragically confused about God's Word and the truth. You *cannot* believe in God's Word, hear Jesus say, "I am the way, the truth, and the life, and nobody comes to the Father but through me," and still believe that "all religions are the same."

Those in leadership desperately need to be plugged into relationships where they are encouraged to tell the truth (the whole truth and nothing but the truth) about themselves, allowing the surgery of God's sharp Word and the healing ointment of Christian love to cure the spiritual ailments that can afflict us all.

A healthy pastor has the ability to go to his board and say, "Friends, I think you're wrong on this, but I'm willing to submit. Let's move forward together." If he can't do that, he needs to leave rather than seek to change the church. His sense of needing to be right every time, his desire to protect his power and authority, must be surrendered to God.

Frequently I hear pastors talk about not being able to be open with anyone. I don't buy it. If I were the pastor of a small-town church, I would do whatever it took to find an accountability partner I could trust. No, I would not confess my sins to another minister in that town and end up as a sermon illustration. No, I would not have someone in my own church or on my elder board be my accountability partner, unless I had worked for several years to build a healthy and authentic church. But a partner is needed. If I had to drive three hours once a week to have such a partner, I would do it. And in my opinion, any pastor must be willing to do the same. If it means hiring a counselor who is bound by law to keep everything confidential, then so be it. Without such a trusted partner, temptation and sin will gain the power to pull the ministry down, or at least prevent it from becoming all it could be. Here is why.

When a secret temptation or obsession plagues a pastor, it gains power in his life. It grows to control him more and more and makes him doubt his salvation and God's love. It walls off his ministry and hardens his heart. The top item on his agenda becomes hiding the secret rather than connecting with God and others. But when a pastor becomes open, sin is revealed and ultimately loses its power. Satan adores the secrets of leaders, because one secret can affect so many. But when a struggler opens up about a sin or a temptation, Satan shrinks, his demons recoil, and the freedom of Christ can once again be celebrated.

Years ago I attended a seminar for leaders where I rededicated my life to the Lord. I turned a great corner and returned home with new enthusiasm to serve the Lord. I put a lot of things together—except for accountability. I did not think I needed it. The power of God in my life was so awesome that I thought it was all I needed! I would be accountable to him alone.

When my closest friends heard of my new dedication, I distanced myself from them in self-righteousness. What felt real and powerful to me soon became a source of pride, and Satan used it to grow superficiality where authenticity was needed.

As you might imagine, it wasn't long before I found myself sliding down my spiritual mountaintop into a pile of temptation. I began to daydream about a young woman at a restaurant (in other words, I lusted after her). I did not want to tell my wife, my friends, or anyone. It was a huge problem, but my pride kept me from seeing the reality of what I was doing. Soon it engulfed me. It was already an affair of the mind and was headed toward an affair of the flesh.

Fortunately, I did not wait any longer. I humbled myself before one of the two men I can approach with my problems and frankly told him of my temptations and vulnerability. Together we developed a plan of accountability. Every day he asked me if I had visited that restaurant or talked to that young woman. Knowing I had to answer his daily questions provided the motivation I needed to cross the line from sin to responsibility. And the power of accountability broke the power of temptation.

Through this incident I came to understand in a new way that "where two or more are gathered together in my name, there I will be also." The might of the Holy Spirit and the strength of a friendship saved me from the path of destruction.

Everyone needs a trusted friend for those times when only a spiritual 911 call will change the course of a heart that's off track.

WARNING: SAINTS UNDER CONSTRUCTION!

You've seen those bright orange, diamond-shaped highway signs that say, "Road Work Ahead." When you see one, you groan a little, tap your brake pedal, and say, "Good grief, what now? Will there be a flagger? Will I have to sit for ten minutes?" Then you see a sign that says, "Highway Under Construction, Next 8 Miles," or something of the sort.

You know what? I think it would be healthy if believers wore diamond-shaped signs around their necks that said, "Have Patience. Believer Under

Construction" or "Proceed Carefully: God's Work Zone." You should see a little orange sign like that when you look in the mirror each morning, so you'll remember to be patient with yourself in all your shortcomings. You should see signs like that when you meet someone in the hallway at school, sit with him at the dinner table, or bump into her at church. We're all under construction. We all have quite a ways to go. None of us is "there" yet. In our lifelong objective to become more and more like God's Son (see Romans 8:29), we're only just getting started. I like the way Paul said it to the church at Philippi:

> I don't mean to say I am perfect. I haven't learned all I should even yet, but I keep working toward that day when I will finally be all that Christ saved me for and wants me to be.
>
> No, dear brothers, I am still not all I should be but I am bringing all my energies to bear on this one thing: Forgetting the past and looking forward to what lies ahead, I strain to reach the end of the race and receive the prize for which God is calling us up to heaven because of what Christ Jesus did for us. (Philippians 3:12-14, TLB)

See what I mean? The orange signs are still up. We're still in a work zone. There is still need for patience. We're still in process. Even the great apostle Paul knew he hadn't (yet) become what he needed to be. We need to draw from our relationship with the Lord in order to build intimacy and authenticity with others. If I come before God every day feeling like a grateful beggar who's been given a gift I could never have earned in a billion years, I am much more likely to see another person as a fellow beggar, rather than as somebody who is too far above me to care or too far beneath me and not worthy of my time. Like the sign in the clubhouse said: Nobody too big, nobody too small. Everybody medium. Everybody "standin' in the need of prayer"—together!

A SAFE PLACE

What do we most need in life? We need healthy relationships that fill us with a sense of significance and a sense of security. We need to matter and to feel safe.

We all need a safe place to express our emotions without having to worry about living up to someone's illegitimate expectations. We need a place where we are free to explore perceptions, thoughts, and feelings. We need a forum where new ideas and new forms of communication can be practiced and supported. We need to feel the freedom to be who we want to be without fear of retribution. We need a safe place where we find relief by saying the tough things rather than holding them in. In other words, we need strong relationships where people are valued over rules or performance.

A safe family is one where a son can come to a father and say, "Dad, I've gotten involved in drugs. I'm scared, and I need your help"—and the father isn't outraged or shocked, but can reply, "I'm here to help you, Son." Such a father loves his son and is terrified for him, but he remains calm in the midst of his son's panic and shame. That father will not throw out his son because he's misbehaved. In a safe family you don't have to perform right to get love and affection; in a safe family you enjoy love and affection even when you mess up. In a safe family, every member can be vulnerable. The family's relationships are valued over all else.

A safe church is one where I can go to the pastor and say, "I'm sinning." In a safe church I can embrace loving discipline without fearing I will be ostracized or condemned. In a safe church people say things like, "We feel bad for you. We are hurt by your behavior—but not embarrassed." In a safe church, relationships clearly are the top priority, and therefore vulnerability is prized, not penalized.

So let me ask: Do you feel that *you* matter? Do *you* feel safe?

And even beyond that—do you help others to feel that they matter? Do you help others to feel safe? That's really the bottom line for a healthy faith, as the apostle Paul makes so clear:

> Let no debt remain outstanding, except the continuing debt to love one another, for he who loves his fellowman has fulfilled the law. (Romans 13:8)

CHAPTER 12

ARE WE THERE YET?

A Healthy Faith Is Growing

But grow in the grace and knowledge of our Lord and Savior Jesus Christ.

2 Peter 3:18

When my daughter, Madeline, was born, we bonded like superglue. I would have walked on hot coals for that baby girl! She could do no wrong. If she threw her milk off the high chair, I would marvel at what a good arm she had—or how artistic the splatters on the wall were. I could hardly believe God had given us such a perfect child.

And then something strange happened. The older she grew, the less perfect she became.

As time went on, what I used to think was cute began to look more and more like meanness, even downright rebellion. There were times when I almost wondered if she were demon possessed. (Where do you find an exorcist in the Yellow Pages?)

Man, this parenting stuff was *tough!* My sense of fun evaporated like spilled Coke on a hot sidewalk. Madeline was causing me major stress by simply being a normal three-year-old, getting into everything and messing up what she got into.

What a disappointment! I didn't want to be Mr. Wonderful Father anymore. I didn't care if I failed to win Father of the Year. *She doesn't deserve my being wonderful,* I thought. *What she really deserves is reform school.* I was burned out.

But not for long.

A wise man came alongside me and taught me a great lesson. "If you give your kids only what they deserve," he told me, "you will rob them of a healthy life. Don't give them what they deserve; give them what they *need.* Just like Jesus does for us!"

Shazam! What a life-changing moment! Jesus does not respond to us based on what we deserve to get. He responds based on what we need. He provides for our needs even though we are undeserving. He died for us while we were still in rebellion against him. He allows us to grow. He does not force us to clean up our act before he comes into our lives. He meets our needs and gives us the grace and the space to grow.

A Humbling Parallel

As I thought about how difficult it was to see Madeline develop some troubling characteristics—even belligerence and rebellion—I suddenly saw the parallel with our Father God and all of his children. Every one of us is rebellious. We pout. We shout "No!" in our spirits. We sneak around doing what we know we ought not to do. And yet he accepts us wherever we are. He refuses to abandon us or give us what we so richly deserve; he pours great rivers of (amazing) grace into our lives. As David marveled,

> He does not treat us as our sins deserve
>> or repay us according to our iniquities.
> For as high as the heavens are above the earth,
>> so great is his love for those who fear him;
> as far as the east is from the west,
>> so far has he removed our transgressions from us.

As a father has compassion on his children,
so the LORD has compassion on those who fear him.
(Psalm 103:10-13)

Thinking about the grace God has given to me has helped me become a grace giver to my daughter. Her imperfections have helped me to see my own. Accepting her as she is has helped me taste the wonder of how God accepts me as I am. And as I've watched her grow physically, I've asked myself, "Am I growing to the same extent spiritually? What is God looking at in my life and saying, 'I wish he wouldn't do that' or 'I understand why he's doing that, but if he wouldn't, he would sure have a better life'?"

I want to see my character develop, just as I am discovering how my daughter's character needs to develop. I see her growing into a wonderful, mature, imperfect human being whom I love to a degree I never thought possible. I have thrilled with a deep sense of pride and delight in her words and her ways. And within that warm glow of love and pride, I dare to believe God cherishes similar feelings about me.

Instead of God shaking his head and muttering, "Why aren't you having a one-hour quiet time every day?" I hear him saying, "Wow! That three minutes with you today was really a rich time, Steve. I'm so glad we could spend it together." More and more through the years, I see God as allowing us to grow, encouraging us to grow, and helping us to grow—even through those inevitable periods of pain and suffering and confusion.

INSTANT MATURITY?

Too often in church we want people to be instantly mature. We want them to clean themselves up if they hope to be with us. But a healthy church takes people in just as they are, broken and dirty, and gives them the freedom to grow. A healthy church doesn't aim to minister only to those who look good, but also to those who have heard the call of the Master, regardless of their life circumstances.

Remember when Jesus went to the little tax collector's house for supper? Zacchaeus was delighted that Jesus came. And sometime during his visit—so criticized by the scandalized Pharisees—that despised little man gave his heart and soul to Jesus Christ. Even before Jesus left his home that day, Zacchaeus began to grow. In front of everybody, he declared, "Look, Lord! Here and now I give half of my possessions to the poor, and if I have cheated anybody out of anything, I will pay back four times the amount" (Luke 19:8).

Can you imagine Jesus walking through Zacchaeus's home that day and saying, "Oh wow, Zacchaeus, you've really been reading some trash. These Roman poets have to go! And that artwork on the walls! It's scandalous! Shame on you! And you've been drinking just a little too much wine, don't you think? Better shape up, Mister, if you want to hang out with me."

Of course not! Jesus celebrated Zacchaeus's new birth and those first baby steps of growth. He knew that more growth would come over time as that new convert walked with God. That was why Jesus sought out Zacchaeus while he was up a tree. He knew the nature of Zach's heart and knew what he was capable of becoming. He knew there was a reason this cheater and thief had gone to a lot of trouble to see him.

Jesus also knows your heart and sees your future, no matter what your reputation has become. He is seeking you out, just as he did Zach—even if you are up a tree.

I love what the apostle Paul once wrote about his efforts to plant a church: "I planted the seed, Apollos watered it, but God made it grow" (1 Corinthians 3:6). Paul knew it wasn't his job to cause growth, so he left that task in the hands of God—the only One capable of successfully pulling it off.

GROWING PAINS

One of my favorite writers is a recovering alcoholic. She's a Christian, but she still struggles with profane language. Words you'd rather not hear sometimes fly out of her mouth. Yet for all of that, her writing is real. I love her honesty! One day someone told me that if this author were really a Christian, she wouldn't talk the way she does. I disagreed. I described my joy that now she talks about Christ instead of discussing drugs, alcohol, and other worldly things. If Christ can bring her up from her cave of depravity, he can also correct her language—in due time. She simply needs an opportunity to grow.

A man named M. R. Siemens well understood this principle. M. R., as he liked to be called, was a "retired" pastor who loved to take the helm of struggling churches and nurture them back to spiritual health. Occasionally a few zealous church members would encourage him to preach against smoking or theater attendance or the like. He never did. Why not? "It seems to me that the Word tells us it's the Holy Spirit's job to convict men and women of sin," he'd say gently in his deep, bass voice. "And so far as I know, he's not unemployed."

Pastor Siemens accepted his people where they were and helped them to grow into mature believers. He didn't threaten. He didn't cajole. He didn't embarrass. He simply preached the Word faithfully, lived out the gospel practically, and let God do his job.

Once he was returning home from an evangelistic campaign in Chetek, Wisconsin, and around midnight came upon a stranded motorist covered in oil and red-faced with anger. M. R. stopped his car and asked how he could help. The fuming man asked for a ride, hopped in, and then let loose with a ten-minute barrage of profanity about his blankety-blank car. When he finished, he turned to the smiling pastor and said, "By the way, what are you doing out so late? What do you do?"

"I'm a pastor, and I'm just returning home from speaking at some evangelistic meetings in Chetek," M. R. answered.

The man was aghast. "Why didn't you stop me?" he exclaimed, embarrassment choking his voice. "A pastor shouldn't hear that kind of stuff."

"Your problem isn't your mouth," M. R. replied kindly. "It's your heart." And he proceeded to lead that man to Christ.

The angels in heaven rejoiced mightily that night because Dr. Siemens refused to let an angry man's vocabulary put him off. "How else should we expect him to speak?" M. R. often asked. "Would it be better for a man to sing hymns all the way to hell?"

We must not demand instant change and quick fixes from those who find their way to Christ. We must allow for a process of transformation and growth. When Christ delivers someone from a sin, he doesn't usually deliver him or her instantly into character. Character takes time to build and grow. God asks us to be patient with his people. Let's allow him to change them through the power of the Holy Spirit. He can accomplish through love and divine wisdom what we can never change through wagging our heads and pointing our fingers.

THE RIGHT SOIL

It is our nature to seek quick relief from pain. But in our fear that we will live in pain forever, or that the pain will overwhelm us, we often run to the closest form of relief. Unfortunately, this tendency does not allow for growth in faith, for life's difficulties are the soil in which great faith grows. When we feel pain and stand firm, trusting that God will see us through, we are rewarded with a strengthened faith that will make the next crisis less traumatic.

Helen Keller once said, "Character cannot be developed in ease and quiet. Only through experience of trial and suffering can the soul be strengthened, vision cleared, ambition inspired, and success achieved." It's when I don't understand life that I am forced to stretch and work out and build up my faith. If everything magically and wonderfully fell into place, I would have no need for God or for Jesus or for a growing faith. It's in those times when life doesn't make sense—when things aren't black and white, when mysteries and perplexities cloud my understanding—that this thing called faith begins to send down its thick, strong roots.

My life is littered with mistakes—the mistakes of others as well as my own. But in every one of those incidents, God came along, picked up the litter, and put it together in a way that made it into a faith monument. I can look back at some of those times and say, "It was at *that* very point, in the midst of *that* adversity, that this part of my character began to grow and my relationship with God really deepened. My faith grew not because God shielded me from struggles and pain, but because he saw me through it all. Because my Lord and I shared in that suffering, our relationship grew stronger."

Without enduring pain, suffering, and adversity, we will know only a shallow faith. I have met some very good people who have lived wonderfully comfortable, predictable lives, and I've found myself saying to friends, "I wonder if their life is too good, too comfortable, too rich, for them ever to sense their need for Jesus." Their faith not only doesn't grow—it never begins.

I can look back now and honestly say I'm grateful for my struggles, for those painful things that fertilized the soil of my faith so that its roots could grow deep. I'm grateful that while I have watched others in the midst of struggle and confusion turn away from faith in Christ, my own faith has grown. What a gift from God!

A friend of mine is a recovering alcoholic. This was a point of great shame in his life, because as a Christian he had to finally admit that yes, he drank; yes, he had a drinking problem; and yes, he needed to enter a recovery program. Once a successful, wealthy salesperson, he watched all his money evaporate because of his drinking and irresponsible behavior.

At the lowest point of his life, in the trench of disgust, he reached up to

God and met Jesus. And in that first year of his recovery, he grew more in character and stature than he had in the previous ten years! Not only was he going to recovery meetings and having his own personal time with the Lord, but he also got involved in a Bible college and plunged into a study of the Scriptures. In one amazing year, he became a true man of God. I watched him move from successful salesperson...to abject, miserable failure...to zealous believer preparing for future ministry. Now he ministers in one of the largest churches in America.

That kind of transformation is what can happen when we finally give up that one thing we've been holding onto most tightly. It's almost as if we spring forth like a stone from a slingshot, right into the arms of the Lord. Then he takes us up, nurtures us through his presence, teaches us life-changing truths, and grows us up in himself more than we could ever have imagined.

When we determine to face the storms of life with only our faith in God and the support of other healthy believers, we set ourselves up for growth. God will take that little acorn of pure faith and grow it into a strong and abiding oak. God does not require a lot of faith to start the growth process; he needs only a little seed of healthy faith. Christ described this small faith as being the size of a mustard seed (Matthew 17:20). From such a small speck of faith, the impossible can be accomplished.

RIGIDITY, THE OPPOSITE OF GROWTH

While Jesus Christ needs only a little seed of healthy faith to start us on the road to spiritual strength, it helps if that seed is planted in rich soil. Rigidity isn't such a fertile soil; it's much too cracked and dry.

Did you know that a child with a rigid parent (or parents) usually enters adulthood clinging to someone serving up any form of rigidity? One would think that the adult child, having escaped such rigidity at home, would forever flee from it. Instead the individual is often drawn to it. Why? One explanation is that human beings are creatures of habit; we take comfort in what we know.

One boy was reared in a rigid household where it was difficult to express who he was or what he wanted. His father communicated with directives, offering no reasons for his demands but expecting immediate compliance. The boy rebelled. He became a heavy drug user, and at age eighteen he quit school to live with several other drug addicts. Eventually his addiction put him out of work, and he found himself at the bottom with no hope.

When a cult follower befriended him, he responded. He felt loved and supported as he heard a genuine offer of help. Inside the cult, he encountered a controlling leader who dictated the group's every decision. The young man had found home. He had come full circle, back to a variation of his original situation. He became a faithful follower, unwilling to question the validity of the group, its rules, or the demands it placed on him.

Another reason we so often choose rigidity over growth is that it's easier. Why struggle over how to respond to a difficult situation when your rigid system gives you every answer ahead of time?

I used to work with a gentleman who was committed to a child-rearing technique focused (supposedly) on how God wants us to rear children. In reality, this system championed how one author *thought* God wanted us to rear our children.

This gentleman's first three children were extremely compliant. When he applied these rigid techniques to those kids, they worked perfectly. (His children were so compliant that I believe any technique would have worked; there wasn't a lot you could do to mess up those kids.) He was proud of the results, and he often insinuated that because I wasn't following that same rigid system, I was making many mistakes. After all, he had the proof: three lovely, compliant children. They confirmed that his system was the only way to go!

Then God blessed his family with a fourth child—and suddenly this man's wonderful, smooth-running system started spinning its wheels. It sputtered, coughed, and died. It simply didn't work. The fourth child flatly (and loudly) declined to comply.

I had to stifle myself one evening when I shared a meal with this man's family. While the three compliant children sat there contentedly eating their preselected meal entrées, the fourth one clenched his teeth and refused to eat a single morsel. Dad wouldn't give him what he wanted, so he WOULD NOT eat! And so we sat, caught in the midst of a great struggle.

Before long, this dad began to abandon parts of his rigid system. He started to sense he needed to pick his battles. He began to raise this boy as an individual, rather than the next uniform cog in the family wheel.

I think God plays tricks on some parents who think they have it all together. He gives them that one child who doesn't fit the formula—or any formula! You have to throw out the notebooks and tapes and charts and start from scratch, depending on the Lord day by day. My formerly smug friend learned that life is not a set of 1-2-3 rules that can be applied in all situations. Rigidity can be a great detriment to us, especially when we try to inflict it on other people as God's will.

A NET GAIN OF ONE STEP

Even though I am a Christian and have surrendered my life to God, the Holy Spirit continues to peel back areas of my heart that need to change and come under his Lordship. Areas of irresponsibility. Areas of immaturity. Areas where I have refused to yield. Areas where I insist on gratifying myself.

Good things happen as I confess these things. When I admit my irresponsibility, opening that area of my life to the scrutiny of God and my accountability partners, I actually begin to grow into responsibility! And the more I grow, the more responsibility God gives me. It thrills me to see him honor that growth.

Years ago when I when I finally came back to the Lord, I began to admit that I had large areas of unforgiveness in my life. I confessed my struggles both to the Lord and to friends, and he went to work on that unyielded ground. He showed me how I needed both to forgive myself for some horrendous things and to accept his forgiveness. He revealed some old, calcified areas of bitterness and unforgiveness in my soul and helped me yield those things.

This didn't happen overnight. In fact, it's still happening. Today I sense more and more freedom and joy where there used to be shadow and denial and hardness.

Friend, a healthy faith is a growing faith, and spiritual growth and character growth are always a process. Like physical conditioning, they don't occur in every life in the same way or at the same pace. There are ups and downs. Sometimes, like the old Swindoll title, it's three steps forward and two steps back.

But that's still a net gain of one step!

CHAPTER 13

SERVICE WITH A SMILE

A Healthy Faith Is Free to Serve

You, my brothers, were called to be free. But do not use your freedom to
indulge the sinful nature; rather, serve one another in love.

Galatians 5:13

As a college student at Baylor University, I had the pleasure of being in a club
with Jay Burns, a young man with brilliance and discipline far beyond my
own. Jay was one of the most well-liked people in school. As a premed student he carried around flashcards to help him memorize the parts of the body
and all the formulae and esoterica he needed to learn for organic chemistry
and biology. He was a great student and creative to boot.

One year Jay and I choreographed a dance number for our club in the
school-wide competition called "Sing." We took fourth place, the highest
spot the club had ever earned before or since. I have fond memories of Jay
Burns.

That's why I was so delighted recently to read in *Dallas Magazine* that Jay
was listed as the top plastic surgeon in town. Not only had he achieved excel-
lence at Baylor, but today other Dallas physicians recognize him as the top
dog in his profession. A person in such a celebrated position could do just
about anything he wanted with his fame and fortune.

But do you know what Jay has chosen to do with it? He often takes his formidable talents and skills on the road to visit Third World countries where he performs plastic surgery on impoverished children. If it weren't for him, those children would have to face difficult lives with gross deformity. But because of Jay, they don't go to the sliding-scale clinic where the ones who barely graduated from medical school are gamely trying to correct ghastly deformities. Instead, they get the very best. Jay freely and willingly serves God in those developing countries by helping children to look normal—sometimes even beautiful.

HE MADE HIMSELF NOTHING

I always am delighted to discover individuals who are able to get out of themselves and into the lives of others. I gleefully celebrate men and women who truly enjoy serving others.

I believe Philippians 2:5-8 lays the foundation for our ability to serve freely: "Your attitude should be the same as that of Christ Jesus: Who, being in very nature God, did not consider equality with God something to be grasped, but made himself nothing, taking the very nature of a servant, being made in human likeness. And being found in appearance as a man, he humbled himself and became obedient to death—even death on a cross!"

God the Father did not force, cajole, or guilt-trip his Son into coming to earth and dying on the cross for us. No, Jesus did it voluntarily, willingly, even eagerly. I love that! Surrounded by the incomprehensible glories of heaven, Jesus pointedly decided not to hold onto his divine position and lofty rights, but instead chose to come and serve us, even to the point of suffering a criminal's death on a Roman cross.

Jesus demonstrates to us that a big part of healthy faith is being free to serve. Both parts of this idea are important to keep together. Believers are *free* to *serve*. Faith systems that coerce their members into service with threats or high-pressure, heap-on-the-guilt methodologies neither honor God nor produce healthy believers. Service is a natural outgrowth of a healthy faith.

And it comes as a free-will offering of the heart.

FREE TO SERVE

A good friend of mine, Kenny Luck, serves his family and his church and also does a tremendous job with us in New Life Ministries. A dedicated father and a loving husband, Kenny enjoys life with a family full of love and fun and excitement—a family most people would envy. He also coteaches a Bible study for men at church. I look at him and see his life, the way he's growing, and I say, "Here's an example of a man committed to serving others in a balanced way."

Above all, God is number one in Kenny's life. His family comes second, his church comes third, and his work comes fourth. And that's the way it should be. Kenny is not at the church twenty hours a week trying to compensate for some hurt or failure in his past. He's not serving so he can feel good about himself or loved by God. He is truly *free* to serve.

How I wish believers like Kenny were the rule! So many men and women are serving because they hope to earn God's favor. They think that if they just do enough, God is going to look down on them and say, "Wow, would you look at that! I've never seen anybody work so hard for me. I think I'm going to give them a million dollars!" Or they hope the Lord will see their hard work and decide to relieve their pain or magically make life easier for them. With their "earn as you go" mentality, they regard their future as being dependent on their ability to achieve, accomplish, and sacrifice. This perspective is characteristic of many religions, though not of true Christianity.

When my wife and I visited Thailand some time ago, we observed hundreds of Buddhist temples and thousands of worshipers practicing their faith. I was overwhelmed by their dedication to their gods. I watched as they bought gold filament and pressed it into a Buddha statue, to the point of causing themselves great physical pain.

We were often confronted with requests to "do something for Buddha." Some wanted us to buy a bird and set it free. Others asked us to give money to restore the temples. We were invited to buy lotus blossoms. All of those things, we were told, would bring us good luck. Worshipers constantly suggested new ways for us to please Buddha and obtain his favor. A person just can't do enough in that land where faith has been replaced by hard work.

Sadly, it is not much different in the United States. Many feel compelled to serve on every church committee or represent the church on every possible community council. Some do this because they hope their work will somehow gain them divine favor. Others do this in an attempt to run from pain. They figure if they can stay busy enough, they will not have to resolve their pain. So they work hard and run fast to stay one step ahead of the hurt.

Those who refuse to risk throwing themselves wholly in the arms of God find it safer to pursue religious activity. For these churchaholics the activity of religion becomes a drug, the quick fix of choice. It appears so admirable, so sacrificial, so exemplary.

How could it be so wrong?

Rather than becoming more filled with the Spirit of God, churchaholics fill their lives with the activities of the church. Rather than becoming more like Christ, they become more like what the church wants them to be—or more like they want to be perceived by others. Nothing is more important to them than their distorted practice of faith. It becomes everything; God and others wind up a distant second.

Just as alcoholics drink to find relief, churchaholics find relief in work. Real people are lost and replaced with those who will help carry out the charade. Busyness becomes the goal and religious compulsivity provides a false presence of God.

Churchaholics have embraced a counterfeit religion. God is not honored, and their relationship with him is not furthered. Rather than running into the loving arms of God, they bury themselves in their compulsive acts. The harder they work, the better they feel because they convince one another that God is applauding their efforts. They are trying to work their way to heaven or pay the price for their guilt—and both attempts are futile. Futile and unnecessary. Christ died on the cross to *free* us from the bondage of having to achieve in order to please God. We do not serve to gain our freedom; we are free, and therefore we serve. As Paul said so eloquently to the believers in Galatia:

> It is for freedom that Christ has set us free. Stand firm, then, and do not let yourselves be burdened again by a yoke of slavery. (Galatians 5:1)

FREE TO *SERVE*

The New Testament insists repeatedly that God's followers are to live in freedom, a freedom that moves us to serve others. Rather than being locked into a confining role or trying to work our way to heaven, we can be free to serve others out of our love for God. Galatians 5:13 declares, "You, my brothers, were called to be free. But do not use your freedom to indulge the sinful nature; rather, serve one another in love."

When many people think of freedom, they think of the liberty to do whatever they please. Some feel a liberty to drink; others feel free to drive expensive cars. But healthy faith does not focus on such trivial things. It does not free us to participate in evil or flirt with sin, but frees us to love each other by serving one another.

If our society has gone over the edge on any one point, it is the emphasis on our own needs, desires, and demands. While we have made great progress over the years in helping people to identify oppressive relationships and motivating them to grow into healthier ones, in the process we have gone too far and encouraged people to focus on themselves, not on others. We have driven people into an obsession with their own needs. Healthy faith reverses this trend and brings a healthy balance back to relationships. Out of a deep faith in and love for God, we are free—not bound!—to serve others.

While the cross is the ultimate example of Christ's service to us, we must remember that Jesus didn't wait until Calvary to begin serving us. He lovingly served his followers throughout his earthly ministry. I don't know of any better picture of true servant leadership than the one in John 13:4-5, where Jesus "got up from the meal, took off his outer clothing, and wrapped a towel around his waist. After that, he poured water into a basin and began to wash his disciples' feet, drying them with the towel that was wrapped around him."

What a picture! The Savior of the world, the God of the universe, got down on his knees to meet one of the basic needs of his disciples! You can't watch Jesus wash the feet of his followers and think that he lorded over his men. Instead, he served them, even washing their filthy feet. And he invites us to follow his example.

SERVE FREELY WHERE YOU'RE GIFTED

We may be free to serve, but how do we know *where* to serve? We get a big clue when we discover our unique gifts and talents. All believers have very real spiritual gifts to minister to others. Paul writes, "Now to each one the manifestation of the Spirit is given for the common good" (1 Corinthians 12:7). Some have the gift of compassion, a supernatural ability to reach out to others and make them feel accepted. Others might have the gift of teaching, causing God's Word to be absorbed into the hearts of their students. Still others may have the gift of leadership or of wisdom or of evangelism. While the gifts differ in function (see Romans 12:6-8; 1 Corinthians 12:7-11; Ephesians 4:11), they have but one common goal: "to prepare God's people for works of service, so that the body of Christ may be built up until we all reach unity in the faith and in the knowledge of the Son of God and become mature, attaining to the whole measure of the fullness of Christ" (Ephesians 4:12-13).

My wife and I have some good friends named Brad and Terri Green. Their first child has twelve different anomalies that are associated with twelve separate syndromes, including severe mental retardation. She's a very disabled girl who needs constant care. Terri has met her daughter's needs and at the same time developed a love for other mothers with children like hers. She loves to volunteer her services to help others. In fact, she was honored in Orange County, California, as the Volunteer of the Year.

Meeting the needs of others seems to come naturally to Terri; she's made it part of her life. It's a gift from God, a supernatural gift. Other mothers might have walked out of the marriage, abandoned the child, or had someone else raise her. But not Terri. She loves to reach out and meet the needs of others.

Some might look at servants like Terri and feel compelled (by a false sense of guilt) to meet the needs of other kids and families, even though they struggle to meet the needs of their own family. If that's who you are, I beg you to stop and evaluate your life's priorities. What are you doing to yourself, your children, and your family for the sake of service? Are you really gifted by God to serve in that way?

For example, I believe home schooling can be a powerful tool when a parent has the necessary skills and talents and organizational abilities. I've seen home-schooled kids who have received the best education available in America. But some parents (who really aren't cut out for it) unwisely choose to home school their kids because some "expert" has convinced them, "This is what a *real* Christian parent does. You have to protect these kids. If you don't do it, nobody will." And they drive themselves (and their children) crazy. They become clinically depressed. And the education their children get is extremely poor.

Why? Because they are trying to do more than they can. They're working outside of their giftedness. And all because they are trying to meet someone else's expectations. God is not honored in such a situation.

If you have been trying to meet the illegitimate expectations of others, no wonder your Christian life is passionless! No wonder you are less interested in serving Christ today than you were two weeks after you became a Christian! The answer to your problem could be (and probably is) discovering what you were created to do. Find your spiritual gift and use it for God. And reignite that old passion!

WHAT ABOUT YOUR OWN NEEDS?

An old joke, though not a very funny one, is full of insight. A mother worked all her life to meet every need of every family member. After her children were grown and out of the house, she was ready for a wonderful life. She had lived for everyone else, and just when she was ready to take time for herself, she died. On her tombstone they wrote, "Now maybe I can get some rest!"

A lot of great moms out there have worked themselves to death meeting everyone else's needs and taking no time for themselves. They see themselves more as slaves to God and family than as free persons equal to others. For them, life is one sacrifice after another. I am sure God will honor such dedication, but I think he would be a lot happier if they would take some time for themselves and enjoy his gift of life. After all, he created them and loves them just as much as those they so incessantly serve.

Modern women feel a lot of pressure. Their grown children leave home later, not marrying until they reach their late twenties. Then, just when a mother finally scoots her children out the door, she often stands there welcoming her mother or father or in-laws into the home. She spends the next ten years playing mother to elderly people, and before it is all done, she has spent 90 percent of her adult life as a caregiver. This role frequently produces anger, depression, and resentment of God and family. A late-in-life nervous breakdown is not uncommon.

One woman described it this way: She was so caught up in meeting other people's needs that if she had a near-death experience, someone else's life would probably flash before her eyes! It does not have to be this way, and thousands are starting to find out there are alternatives to such *de facto* slavery.

It is healthy to recognize we all have some basic needs. What good does it do to meet the needs of others if doing so makes you so angry that you cannot relate to them lovingly? Why should a person work hard for others if the end result is exhaustion and depression, disabling the person and causing a break with reality? Each helping heart must assess its own needs and determine if some have been neglected in ways that could cause major problems later on. God does not love the rest of the world more than he loves you. He loves you, too, he knows your needs, and he wants to see them met. Jesus himself, speaking of life's basic necessities, told us, "Your heavenly Father knows that you need them" (Matthew 6:32).

Christ came to serve people, yet he took time to maintain his health so he could meet others' needs. He took time to eat. He took time to rest. He took time to pray. He could not go on until his own needs were met. He spent time alone, away from the crowds. He relaxed in the homes of close friends.

Today Jesus calls his followers to serve others as he did. He desires for all of us a place of rest and a time to regain perspective. If you do not have that time because you feel driven to meet the needs of everyone else, take a second look at where you are. If you are angry, exhausted, and depressed, take the time to back away and find the rest God wants for you.

I know some churches appear to teach that any type of self-care is selfishness, that any sense of self-awareness is self-absorption. But this is nonsense. You must take time to meet your own needs, just as Jesus took time for himself apart from his disciples.

HEALTHY CHURCH SERVICE

When we choose an opportunity for service in our churches, we ought to do it to honor the Lord, not out of obligation or in an attempt to prove our worth. Service in a church isn't something to be demanded but something believers must feel free to offer. Never should service be coerced.

Sadly, many churches ask people to serve in unhealthy ways. They use force, guilt, manipulation, and other kinds of improper pressure. They will say things like this:

- "If Jesus were in this Sunday school class, *then* would you want to be the teacher?"
- "If I were calling Jesus, do you think *he* would say no to the needs of these children?"
- "You know, the church is not there just to meet your needs. You need to meet the needs of the church."
- "Do you know you are the only person from your neighborhood who is not actively involved in some church ministry?"

When you hear statements like that at church for an extended period of time, watch out! That's manipulation, not the Holy Spirit, and it indicates religious illness, not spiritual health.

Unhealthy churches demand that their members serve, serve, and serve some more. Many unfortunate believers respond by getting involved in countless groups, committees, and meetings. They are pushed to sign up, and they sacrifice their families and friends to meet the church's needs.

This excessive level of service soon becomes overwhelming. Individuals become so drained they can't think clearly. Their emotions become distorted. They slide into deep depression, extreme anxiety, and a general numbness. Activity dries up their soul, leaving many feeling hopeless. Some become victims of total breakdowns. Overwhelming service doesn't put anyone in the spiritual hall of fame; it only puts them in the hospital or destroys their relationships.

Sandy and I once attended a church where we suffered tremendous abuse. Tired and burned out from the unsavory experience, we wanted to flee to a healthy church and be still for a while; we just weren't up to serving. When we met the pastor, Denny Belessi, he somehow knew how to meet our need. "If you like this church and you want to start attending," he said warmly, "then we hope you would just sit back and be ministered to. Take some time to heal."

How refreshing! How freeing! We took him up on his offer, and our faith was restored and rebuilt.

The other day I was talking to Sally, a dear friend from high school. She told me she had been asked to teach a Bible Study Fellowship class in her town. She gave many excuses why she couldn't: She wanted to take her walks in the morning; she would have to give up many other activities she wanted to pursue; etc. The BSF leaders graciously accepted her refusal, but the Holy Spirit continued to impress upon Sally that she could do this, that she was gifted for it, and that it would mean a lot to many women. Finally she reversed herself and said yes.

I think that is so healthy! BSF asked Sally to teach; she said no; they accepted her answer; and then the Holy Spirit moved in her heart to confirm this was something she really ought to do. No high pressure. No guilt. No manipulation. Just a dependence on the Holy Spirit to do his good work.

HAPPY TO SERVE

The church I attend doesn't pressure people to minister but presents many opportunities for service—some 160 active ministries at last count. Most people who start coming to Saddleback move from merely attending to learning and discovering their gifts and strengths, and finally to serving. So when somebody steps up and says, "I feel a need to create a tennis shoe ministry, to take good-but-used shoes down to Mexico and give them to the kids who have none," all of a sudden we have our ministry number 161, called the

Tennis Shoe Ministry. How does it happen? The Holy Spirit instills a passion in someone's heart to go out and reach others in a certain way.

From time to time I get to preach at Saddleback. Sometimes our pastor, Rick Warren, gets sick on Friday, and I'll be asked to preach to fifteen thousand people on Saturday and Sunday. No one has ever asked me, "What are your credentials? Where did you go to seminary?" They just know God has allowed me to serve him through public speaking, so they make the pulpit available to me. I don't know of any place I've ever preached where I've felt the Holy Spirit's presence as much as at Saddleback. It is a healthy church where people are free to serve and use their gifts and talents for the Lord.

Free to serve. To paraphrase the old TV ad, "It don't get much better than that."

CHAPTER 14

ONLY ONE THING
IS NEEDED

A Healthy Faith Is Contented

Keep your lives free from the love of money and be content with what
you have, because God has said, "Never will I leave you; never will I forsake you."

Hebrews 13:5

I've worked for some tough bosses in my life. I've tried to please managers
who could never be pleased. And I've labored to get on the good side of
supervisors only to learn they didn't *have* a good side!

But through my years of life, I've never labored under more relentless
slave drivers than those twin tyrants Greed and Envy. Once you place those
two in positions of upper management in your life, you will never rest again.
They will drive you day and night.

Unhealthy faith draws its poison from the gnarled, ancient roots of
greed and covetousness. As with the money-changers described in Matthew
21:12-13, those who operate in a toxic faith system think nothing of using
the hard-earned sacrifices of others for their own profit and pleasure—and all
in the name of God, of course! Unhealthy faith promotes the excesses of

materialism over good stewardship. It embraces worldly standards of success over the spiritual concept of godliness. And ultimately, it kills.

NO ROOM FOR TWO MASTERS

Healthy faith does not try to serve two masters, for it's impossible. Jesus said clearly, "No servant can serve two masters.... You cannot serve both God and Money" (Luke 16:13).

It was true then, and it is oh so true now. We tend to think of greed just in financial, Ebenezer Scrooge terms, but it has many subtle manifestations. Greed for power. For position. For popularity.

Politicians may be greedy for press coverage. Students may be greedy for attention and the approval of some elite group. Authors may be greedy for reviews of their books and invitations to TV and radio talk shows. Pastors may be greedy to hit a certain attendance number, thinking of the prestige, rather than the people. Any form of greed will eventually consume its owner. It's like owning a pit bull that takes a bite out of you every night until finally there is nothing of "you" left; it's all pit bull.

It's no way to run a healthy Christian life. What does the Scripture say? "But godliness with contentment is great gain" (1 Timothy 6:6).

Great gain!

I like that. It isn't a small gain or a temporary gain or a quick high that leaves you flat. "Great" is a translation of the Greek word *megas,* which may be rendered "exceedingly great, greatest, high, large, or, mighty."

If you are a custodian and you are living a godly, contented life, that is a HUGE gain for you. It is a gain of mighty and eternal proportions. It's not just okay; it is a gargantuan thing. There's no envy, no sense of, "If I only had that position, that job, or more education, I would be more useful in the eyes of heaven."

Remember those tough bosses I mentioned a few paragraphs back? After finally working up the courage to give my notice to one of those guys, I remember the sweet sense of exaltation and relief that swept through me when I walked away from his office. I was unemployed and nearly broke, but I was *free!* In the same way, a faith finally free from playing the comparison game is peaceful, calm, open to direction—and a wonderful place to rest.

DON'T WEAR YOURSELF OUT

Solomon wrote: "Do not wear yourself out to get rich; have the wisdom to show restraint" (Proverbs 23:4). In my own experience, I've found there is only one way to protect yourself from being consumed by greed, and that is understanding where all money comes from—God—and giving a portion back to him out of gratitude for all of it. All the money I make is God's money, so why should it be a problem to give a tithe back to him plus a portion that I call the offering? It all belongs to him. The whole enchilada. He just lets me use some of it to meet needs (and satisfy a few wants as well).

I started my career in the psychiatric health care industry, providing Christian treatment to people with psychiatric and emotional problems. So many of the people who preceded me in this industry have since become multimillionaires. I'm probably one of the few who never got wealthy. But I have never been angry or resentful about that, because I have something far better than a million dollars. I have contentment in my heart. I'm happy for the ministry God gave me, and I will share with anyone who wants to listen story after story of how God has so generously provided for our needs through the years.

I have many flaws and defects, but I am glad to be known for being generous in negotiation and deals. Just the other day, someone was telling me I shouldn't get involved in negotiations because I tend to want to give everything away. I can truly testify that the happier and more fulfilled I have been in my walk with Christ, the less occasion I have found to worry or concern myself with money.

Sadly, many people in ministry start out with those sorts of attitudes, but get more and more concerned about money as time goes by. Between publishing contracts and speaking fees and other sources of revenue, they become wealthy, acquiring the inevitable burdens and baggage of wealth.

Guess what happens then? They begin to lose the joy of helping people. Ministry becomes a bother or a chore, rather than a consummate delight. As Solomon warned, they begin to wear themselves out. It usually isn't long before their ministry loses its effectiveness and they begin to misrepresent God.

The apostle Paul knew about that. With heaviness in his heart, the faithful old warrior told Timothy, "Please come as soon as you can, for Demas has left me. He loved the good things of this life and went to Thessalonica" (2 Timothy 4:9-10, TLB).

I have worked with people who felt God used money in their lives like lollipops—if he loved them, he gave them money, and if he was angry with them, he took the money away. They locked into a system that made them greedy and focused on material things, believing them to be a mark of God's favor.

You and I have to accept the certainty that material prosperity is only temporary. We have to develop, as Paul did in Philippians 4:11, a contentment in whatever circumstances we find ourselves, trusting that God has given us what he intends for us to have.

Paul, of course, got this attitude from his Lord. And in Matthew 6:33, our Lord tells us, "But seek first his kingdom and his righteousness, and all these things will be given to you as well." If we don't seek God's kingdom first, we may find ourselves adding some things that God didn't intend for us to have. Many people are praising God for financial blessings that in reality were delivered by Satan to try to gain control over their lives. We need to be aware that the devil will use anything he can to tear us away from allegiance to the Christ he so bitterly hates. Money is one of his most effective tools.

Just the other day I was walking along the shoreline in my hometown of Laguna Beach. At the moment I was praying, "Thank you, God, for all of your blessings," I looked down and spotted a wet five-dollar bill that had washed up in the white foam of the surf. A grin lit up my face as I picked it up. I thought God must have a sense of humor to show me a five-dollar bill right when I was thanking him for all he has done for me.

But...if there was one five-dollar bill, couldn't there be more? I quickly recalled a time in Hawaii when I found a ten-dollar bill floating in the water, then another and another. Before I was finished on that day I had collected $130. So I began to search the surf for more money. Nothing. Then it hit me. That five-dollar bill was not necessarily a gift from God. It could have been Satan who placed that little fiver before me—or it could have been just one of those things that sometimes happens in life. Wherever it came from, it stopped my time of prayer with God and got me on a search for money.

That leads me to the big question. Since money so often destroys a relationship between us and God, why would God give it to those who cannot handle it? Just like my little find on the beach, Satan may be at the heart of some of our financial boons. The devil doesn't care if we're wealthy in the things of this world, so long as we're paupers in our relationship with God.

A GOOD BAROMETER

I think a good barometer of one's faith is one's attitude toward money and possessions. Contrary to what has been so frequently taught in churches and over the airwaves, material blessing is not a sure sign of spiritual strength. This unhealthy belief is largely a reflection of our affluent society that measures people by the amount of money they make. Those who have much want to believe it is a result of God's blessing, a reward for their strong faith.

A physician I know once stated that his house and cars and booming practice were the results of God's rewarding him for his faithfulness. This wonderful Christian had been tainted by his own materialistic lifestyle. Those who get puffed up over all they own should reevaluate the lives of the truly faithful who live in poverty and inconvenience so they can serve others. Wealth is not a certain reward for faithfulness or spiritual strength.

Before Sandy and I were married, we took a missions trip to India. There we met the most Christlike person either of us has ever known, a physician practicing out of the Baptist Hospital in Bangalore, India. When he realized how many mentally ill people needed care, he went back to school after his children had been reared and obtained a degree in psychiatry. He then started a counseling center next to a Methodist church where he would see people free of charge if they had no money.

While psychiatrists around the world drive expensive sports cars or are squired around town in chauffeured limousines, he drove a jalopy that had to be pushed to start. The only thing that worked consistently was its horn. On Sundays he would go to a small church in the slums just outside town and hold a service for faithful believers. We went with him one Sunday to participate in the service.

The church met in a small lean-to shack made of scrap boards and raw lumber. As the hot sun beat down on its roof, the flimsy building turned into a burning oven made more uncomfortable by extreme humidity. To make conditions worse, open sewers outside pumped billows of odors through the church walls.

Into this mat-covered room the faithful walked, limped, and dragged themselves to worship. No one made more than one hundred dollars a month; most made nothing. It was poverty at its most extreme. The people listened to the sermon, sang, prayed, and had Communion.

Then they did an astonishing thing.

They gave their money.

They gave little (since they had almost nothing), but the percentage of their earnings that went to God was extraordinarily high. Although they were barely able to feed their families, their donations signaled massive spiritual strength.

Now if God really blesses people materially for their faithfulness, then that slum should have miraculously turned into a row of mansions—or at least a subdivision of sleek tract houses. But it never did. Why not? Because faith does not work that way.

Our doctor friend did whatever he could to serve people in need. While others sit through retirement, he and his wife formed a wonderful ministry team. His godliness, wisdom and insight eclipse that of anyone I know—yet he lived in a small house that lacked hot running water. Material blessings did not come his way, but I have a hard time imagining what he could do to increase his faith.

The truth is that many have more money, but few are closer to God than this faithful doctor.

If you have accepted the false teaching that the more faithful you are, the greater the material blessing you will receive, you can look forward to great disappointment. In my experience, greater faith has often brought an end to financial wealth. God often chooses to temper a faithful follower in the fires of loss and financial poverty (think of Job). Such experiences seem to prove that when all you have left is God, you get as much of God as you possibly can.

Wealth, of course, is neither bad nor good. It can be both a dangerous, Christian-eating trap and a great blessing with the capacity to advance the kingdom of Christ. Wealth is many things to many people, but one thing it is not is an infallible indicator of spiritual strength.

Don't let anyone tell you otherwise. Don't let anyone rob you of your joy.

YET ANOTHER BIBLICAL PARADOX

Those who have fallen prey to Greed and Envy (and their adopted sister, Discontentment) find themselves saddled with an unquenchable thirst.

Nothing helps. Nothing satisfies. Nothing brings peace. What a terrible way to live! Once we finally break free of those compulsions by resting in and surrendering to the Lord, we no longer need recognition or status to feel okay about who we are. Ironically, it is only when we are truly at peace about where we are and who we are, that we are free to move on or step into greater responsibility within the kingdom of God.

Scripture is chock-full of such paradoxes. The Spirit of God seems to take special delight in turning the world's logic and wisdom on its head. Those who are last will be first. The meek will inherit the earth. Those who surrender everything possess everything. And then the thought embodied in this chapter: those who choose to be content with their station in life, who concentrate on godliness rather than on looking out for number one, will experience great gain and position themselves for vast usefulness in Christ's eternal kingdom. Don't believe me? Then listen to Christ himself:

> "I tell you the truth," Jesus replied, "no one who has left home
> or brothers or sisters or mother or father or children or fields
> for me and the gospel will fail to receive a hundred times as
> much in this present age (homes, brothers, sisters, mothers,
> children and fields—and with them, persecutions) and in the
> age to come, eternal life. But many who are first will be last,
> and the last first." (Mark 10:29-31)

The most satisfying thing about this realization is that you and I don't have to wait for fulfillment. We don't have to wait for our ship to come in or our lottery ticket to deliver millions. We can have all that is really worth having right now! Real peace of heart. Rest. Security. Significance. Teamwork. Affirmation. Joy. All of these things come from the hand of God himself, worked out among his people regardless of our circumstances.

So many men and women all over the world will go to bed tonight feeling unhappy and unfulfilled. They will tell themselves that contentment awaits just around the corner after they have landed the prestigious job... after they have found a mate...after they have a child...after they have published a book...after they have finished an academic program...after they lose that twenty pounds...after they have won a varsity letter...after they get that medal the military denied them years ago...after they drive home with a new Lexus. Yet strangely, even after they achieve some of those very things, they will feel even emptier, even more unhappy.

I can't help but think of our Lord's gentle rebuke for busy, harassed, stressed-out Martha. Remember what he said? "Martha, Martha,...you are worried and upset about many things, but only one thing is needed" (Luke 10:41-42).

Can you believe that? Do you believe that? *Only one thing is needed!* Only one focus. Peace is not "somewhere out there." Peace is right here, right now, this very minute, in our relationship with Jesus Christ. It's available to you in full. Right now. No waiting. No educational, financial, social, or academic preconditions. You don't have to wait until tomorrow when you're a pastor or a pastor's wife or a mother or you hold a master's in theology or you gain some sought-after spiritual gift. And you can find it precisely where Martha's sister Mary found it: at the feet of Jesus.

IS IT FIRE IN THE BELLY OR JUST PLAIN ULCERS?

"Ah," someone will say with a knowing nod. "What you are calling 'peace' is really only a lack of drive and ambition. You gotta have a fire in your belly to get anywhere in this world."

Really? But then what happens to contentment—the very thing Scripture says will bring great gain to our lives?

I [Jack] have a brother-in-law who pastors a small church in upstate New York. His small fellowship has some opportunities to grow, for which he's excited. He stays open to all the options. But he certainly hasn't hung his contentment or joy upon some arbitrary future attendance number.

My brother-in-law is a rare commodity in this cynical world of ours: He's a happy man. His life exudes peace. He truly loves doing what he is doing and where he is doing it. He likes getting up each morning, and he feels satisfied when he lays his head on the pillow each night. If he had some great opportunity or an open door in the future, I'm sure he would check it out. But I can tell you this: He's not watching his mailbox. He's not sitting around waiting for his phone to ring. He's living life to the full right now. He's content. And he is already experiencing great gain.

What's the difference, then, between peace and lack of ambition? I think it boils down to a matter of focus. The difference is a close, personal, day-by-day walk with the living God. If you have that, my friend, you really don't need a lot of trophies, slaps on the back, or a file of press clippings.

I think of Enoch. He achieved something only one other man in all the biblical record accomplished: He walked straight out of this life and into the next without passing through death. I think Scripture implies that this man was so wrapped up in his relationship with the Lord—so accustomed to walking with God in intimate fellowship—that he mostly forgot about his surroundings. He and the Lord continued in their animated conversation right out of this life and into the next. I doubt old Enoch even noticed. I don't think he so much as stuttered, stumbled, or missed a beat. He was so delighted with his relationship with God that what his fellowmen may or may not have been saying about him didn't really matter. In the opinion of his neighbor, brother-in-law, and the butcher on the corner, Enoch may have lacked ambition. But from heaven's perspective, he was the most upwardly mobile man who ever lived!

> By faith Enoch was taken from this life, so that he did not
> experience death; he could not be found, because God had
> taken him away. For before he was taken, he was commended
> as one who pleased God. (Hebrews 11:5)

When you know you are in intimate fellowship with God, there is a sweet contentment in your soul that remains untouched by the external circumstances that bedevil those around you.

CHALLENGE IS A GOOD THING

Of course, a healthy church might indeed occasionally challenge your attitude of contentment. You might be asked, "Are you *sure* this is where God wants you to be?" A loving accountability partner might press you and say, "Are you *sure* you are feeling God's contentment—or could it be you're just afraid to step out on faith into some new areas of ministry?"

That kind of challenge is good. As the book of Hebrews affirms, we must "consider how we may spur one another on toward love and good deeds" (Hebrews 10:24). That sort of interaction is healthy and right.

On the other hand, be wary of those who delight to give you a "thus saith the Lord" statement as if he or she has some sort of inside track on God's will for your life. During this age of grace, God says all believers are members of a "royal priesthood" (1 Peter 2:9) and he insists that all of us have his "anointing" (1 John 2:20,27). We do not need to depend on someone with a special pipeline to God in order to discover his will for us. So beware of those who want to rent you some length of pipe!

IT MAKES NO SENSE

When it comes right down to it, neither greed nor envy makes the least bit of sense for the Christian. They're just illogical. Oh, greed and envy might indeed make sense for the man or woman without God. In an unsavory sort of way, those traits might actually boost the earthly fortunes of someone living without hope of an eternity in heaven with Christ. But for a Christian?

"Keep your lives free from the love of money and be content with what you have," said the writer to the Hebrews, "because God has said, 'Never will I leave you; never will I forsake you'" (13:5).

God counsels us, in effect, "Don't spend your life envying what others have. Why deplete your energy greedily scheming to acquire the next bauble or the latest trinket? Even in this life, they can all be taken from you. You can lose them overnight. And anyway, one day soon I'm going to roll up this universe like a scroll, the heavens will disappear with a roar, the elements will be destroyed by fire, and the earth and everything in it will be laid bare. And then all you ever envied and all that ever excited your greed will instantly disappear—gone forever!"

What will never disappear, however—what can never be gone for even a fleeting instant—is the hand of our God in our own hand as we stroll together into a breathtaking, brilliant eternity. "Never will I leave you," he whispers, "never will I forsake you."

Who needs greed when you've got God?

CHAPTER 15

SWEET EQUILIBRIUM

A Healthy Faith Is Balanced

The man who fears God will avoid all extremes.
Ecclesiastes 7:18

Balance. It's a beautiful thing.

It is also an extraordinarily difficult quality to fake. You can counterfeit a great many attitudes and actions. You can use the right words and adopt the appropriate facial expressions; you can work yourself up into a holy glow. But a healthy, consistent balance? How do you manufacture such a trait? I mean, you either have it or—quite obviously—you don't. And if you do, it is most likely the work of the Holy Spirit in your life.

- I may talk endlessly about myself and my accomplishments, or I make a great show of my humility…but a healthy self-concept that vigorously encourages others is clear evidence of God's presence in my life.
- I may shade or compromise the truth in order to please you and appear loving, or I may beat you about the head and shoulders with the hard edge of Scripture…but a faith that balances truth and love to bring about mutual edification and submission one to another is the fingerprint of God.

- I may proclaim myself tolerant and broad-minded, refusing to pass judgment on a culture that has rejected Christ and embraced all manner of perversions, or I may mock and rail at those who are blinded by Satan and in bondage to sin…but an active compassion that seeks friendship with lost individuals, remembering that I have my own struggles with the flesh, is nothing less than the work of the Holy Spirit in my heart.
- I may glory in my reasoned, educated, intellectual approach to the Christian life, or I may insist on an experiential, emotional expression of the Christ-life within me…but a daily walk with Jesus that is both rooted in Scripture and responsive to the still, small voice of the Spirit is an example of God's own handiwork in a human soul.
- I may be a type-A, take-charge leader who can ram an agenda down the throats of the most recalcitrant committee, or I may be a passive, go-along-to-get-along type who would rather switch than fight every time…but a humble, patient leader who knows how to move a flock from one pasture to the next without sacrificing half of the sheep in the process is something only God can create.

You see? How do you feign a character quality like balance? You might masquerade as a football tight end or a soccer goalie and get away with it for a period or two. But an impostor wouldn't last one minute on the balance beam! Your balance shows who you really are underneath the posturing and the mantra of memorized phrases. For this reason, I believe balance to be a true bellwether among all the traits of a healthy faith—and one of the quickest ways I can think of to spot a practitioner of unhealthy, toxic religion.

STEEL SHEATHED WITH COMPASSION

A balanced person is tolerant and patient, confrontive without being aggressive, assertive without being insensitive, loving and merciful while speaking the plain, unvarnished truth, one who faithfully applies biblical principles to daily living without being preachy or moralistic.

A balanced person knows the difference between having great compassion for someone who drinks because he was abused as child and refusing to hold that individual accountable for his actions. We have compassion, but it is a compassion fortified with steel: It is mercy and grace standing firmly on the side of truth and personal accountability.

How then would a balanced person lovingly confront someone in the church? It's not just a matter of pointing out a biblical wrong. Most folks already know they have done or are doing wrong. The reason you confront is to help people to see how their actions are hurting others—how their behavior goes beyond being wrong "just because the Bible says so." They're also hurting people who love them! They need to see that. They're not only angering God, but they're also hurting his heart—like a father who sees his deeply loved son slipping into drug addiction. They are grieving the Holy Spirit of God, and that grief is real.

My [Jack's] pastor is a concerned and caring shepherd who lets you know he'll be there for you. But when he is there for you, when he's sitting beside you and looking you eyeball to eyeball, he will also tell you, "This behavior is hurting you, your relationship with God, your relationship with the people around you, and it's hurting my heart as your pastor. But I love you enough to stay here anyway. Your sin does not offend me; it breaks my heart."

A balanced faith is not so preoccupied with work that the family is destroyed. It is not so intent on witnessing to unbelievers that it fails to recognize their other legitimate needs. It does not become so involved with memorizing Scripture that the Author of Scripture gets forgotten. Obedience to rules is balanced with freedom to serve others in a thousand different ways.

Do you see what we're talking about here? It is nothing less than the balance of grace and truth. And who does that make you think of?

THE BALANCE OF GRACE AND TRUTH

Only one man who walked this earth held grace and truth in perfect balance. John said of the Lord Jesus that he was "full of grace and truth" (John 1:14). Almost in the next breath, the writer affirmed that while the law came through Moses, grace and truth came through Jesus Christ (John 1:17).

Our Lord is the very embodiment of truth. He told his disciples, "I am the way and the truth and the life" (John 14:6). Yet the same writer also affirms, "From the fullness of his grace we have all received one blessing after another" (1:16).

In other words, Jesus Christ held grace and truth in dynamic tension, in perfect balance. Those who claimed to have a corner on truth found him shockingly overgracious (for example, Nicodemus). Those who hoped for a bit of grace to get them off the truth hook found him unrelenting (for example, the rich young ruler). Jesus held grace and truth in perfect balance because he was and is the perfect man.

If we would be balanced, we must be more like Jesus. If we would be full of grace and truth, in perfect balance and proportion, we must be full of him.

If I present only truth to someone who is vehemently pro-choice, I will only increase their anger and alienation. But if I also communicate to them the grace that God offers them, I have a chance of winning that person to the Lord. If all I do is shame a person who is involved in immoral behavior, whether it's adultery or homosexual acts, then I am not going to connect with that person. But if I can show them some grace for their situation, that there is a light beyond the shame, then I have a greater chance of helping them grab hold of the transforming love of Christ. If all I ever do is reject the alcoholic or snub the divorcee, then I'm not presenting truth with grace as Jesus did. All I'm really doing is presenting truth because it makes me feel smug.

I need to present not merely the truth, but also the grace that motivates people to take a second look at who God is and how much he loves them. Grace shows people the way to God and a loving relationship with him.

You Can't Fake It

Throughout my years of working with people trapped in unhealthy faith systems, I have found lack of balance to be the most obvious and glaring tip-off that someone has slidden into toxic teachings. As I have said, you just can't fake balance. You can't paste it on when you get up in the morning. You can't achieve it by rote memory, and you can't learn it through imitation. Balance requires an inner spiritual equilibrium that proceeds from the Spirit himself.

Toxic faith is generally based on "either-or," "black or white," "us versus them," and "all or nothing" mentalities. There is no room for compromise, no middle ground for those outside the system. Healthy faith accepts that life is not usually black or white and allows the believer to feel okay about struggling with the many gray areas of life. It also rejects the "us versus them" mentality.

I believe this combative mentality pushes many people away from Christianity. Some of our non-Christian friends have told us that the only other Christians they know constantly put down people of other faiths. They make comments about how stupid they are, how misguided their way of life is. What a sad way of expressing Christ's love!

A person with healthy faith can draw people to Christ by refusing to put down other people's beliefs while also refusing to compromise the truth. A healthier approach would be to say something like the following:

"I can understand how people get involved in other religions. Every religion offers something appealing. The fact that so many people are involved in so many religions shows that most everyone is searching for truth and a connection with the Creator of the universe. I have always respected the dedication of the Buddhist monks. I have admired the missionary mind-set of many other faiths. Some of the most wonderful people in my life have been strong adherents of the Jewish faith. I appreciate the things that many religions stand for. Fortunately, I was able to study most of these religions while in seminary.

"One of the things that comes through pretty strongly in these other religions is the need to work your way to God. Your performance means everything. You will commonly hear people of other faiths say that if a person lives a good life, they will gain eternal life or make it into heaven. When I look at my life, I know that I am not a good person. I do some good things (or at least some things that look good). But when I compare myself to God and the example that Jesus set for all of us, I come up way too short to make it to heaven. When I consider the things in my heart and my less-than-noble motives and all the times I have blown it, it is no wonder that I find Christianity so appealing!

"In Christianity, rather than us working our way to heaven, God works his way to us. He sent his Son, Jesus, to do for us what we could not do for ourselves. We can't be good enough for God. We all mess up and sin. I know I do! So Jesus came and showed us how to live, but he also died with the weight of our sinfulness on his shoulders. He came to earth, was crucified, and rose from the grave so that we could be with God. God is holy, we are not, and Jesus forms the bridge between the two.

"Right before Jesus died on the cross, he showed us that believing in him and accepting him as Savior is all we have to do to gain eternal life. The thief on the cross next to Jesus was anything but good, but he came to believe Jesus was the Savior of the world just before he died. Jesus told him that he would be in paradise with him that very day.

"So I don't have to be good to get into heaven. When I really understood God's grace, I became motivated to honor his gift and be the best man I can be. It is amazing how much easier and enjoyable it is to do good things for others when the pressure to earn your way to heaven is taken away.

"It is sad that your friends put down everyone who is not a Christian, because we are all in this together. We are all searching for truth and seeking to have a relationship with God. I hope that others, who are focused on being good, discover that it is in Jesus that we find both."

In this example there is no put-down, just the reality of what I have found in my search. A lot of this makes sense to most people. When we abandon the "us versus them" mentality, people are drawn to us and to Christ. The person with healthy faith sees himself or herself as part of a greater community in which all of us are struggling with our relationships with our God, our fellow human beings, and ourselves.

Where healthy faith grows, every area of the believer's life improves. In the balanced practice of the Christian faith, families grow closer, friendships become stronger, and conflict gets resolved more easily. The focus is on God, and the individual is seen as a valuable creation of God, worthy of God's attention. Rigidity is replaced with understanding. Those who grow in the faith find comfort because their lives regain perspective. They find wholeness in their balanced faith.

My wife is a wonderful example of a balanced Christian. She loves the Lord with all her heart and serves him vigorously, but she has somehow kept up all her friendships with non-Christian women. When she uses Scripture in her conversations, she uses it to connect with individuals, rather than alienating them or driving them away. I believe she's got the balance down; she's sensitive to people's personal needs as well as their need for truth. Again, it is the balance of grace and truth. That's the balance we as believers need.

AVOIDING EXTREMES

Balance is not well served by extremes. A friend of mine understands this well.

My friend was suffering from high blood pressure and thought he would soothe his frayed nerves by purchasing a tropical fish aquarium. It really wasn't a good idea. What he actually discovered was fourteen ways to kill off the exotic little creatures. If it wasn't the water temperature, it was the pH level. If it wasn't the chlorine, it was something else. Every morning he would find another corpse floating in the tank, and his blood pressure got nothing but worse until he trashed the whole affair.

Tropical fish don't like extremes. It turns their tank toxic.

People don't do well with extremes either. When we tell ourselves that people and issues can be viewed totally in terms of white or black, all good or all bad, completely right or completely wrong, we drive ourselves to fuel crusades against "the corrupt."

And that's not all. When we see everything in extremes, we often end up denying our errors. Why? Because just one mistake makes us feel like a failure. So we begin to deny the existence of even small problems in an effort to defend against feelings of total failure.

People will comment, "I don't understand why that man cannot admit even one mistake." Why can't he? Because if he admits a single mistake, he will feel like a complete failure; he will believe he is capable only of making mistakes. So denial becomes his defense. The individual denies the one extreme of bad and creates the illusion of living at the opposite extreme of perfection.

The only way to help people recover from such an unhealthy faith is to confront that kind of thinking. They must be told over and over that making a mistake does not make *them* mistakes or failures. Additionally, another person who makes one mistake or disappoints them in one way is not all bad. There are still some wonderful things about that person.

Sin is an act; it is not a description of every facet of one's character. You do not have to be perfect to be good. You do not have to be perfect to be accepted. God does not accept you based on a perfect performance, and it is futile to attempt to gain further acceptance from him. God is interested in relationship with you, not in your working and trying harder to earn his love.

God cares about you. *You*, with all of your imperfections, are the focus of God's love. These thoughts must replace the extremes of toxic thinking.

Christ himself spoke of resisting the urge to view things in terms of extremes. When confronted about breaking a law on the Sabbath, he told his critics that he desired mercy rather than sacrifice (see Matthew 12:7).

Pure faith is a faith of mercy. We have the benefit of a merciful God. We must incorporate that mercy into our views of other people and ourselves. Doing so can bring us great relief and begin the process of reestablishing relationships that had been damaged by thinking in extremes. A truly biblical, Spirit-filled faith will display an attractive, winsome balance that draws people in rather than drives them away.

THE IMBALANCE OF PASSIVITY

If some of us err on the side of perfectionism and workaholism, others of us err on the side of passivity. A passive believer repeats to himself: Having true faith means waiting for God to help me—and doing nothing until he does!

This belief is a foundation for disaster. I have seen many people experience deep hurt as they waited around for God to do something that God expected *them* to do. Wives of alcoholics allow drinking to continue when taking the steps to intervene would reverse the course of the problem. Church leaders allow a minister to crash and burn under the influence of sex, silver, or self-obsession. They pray God will change him when they need to exercise the tough side of love and confront the person about his or her character defects. Parents allow a child to grow up spoiled and immature, praying that God will protect him rather than forcing the child to take responsibility for himself.

Too often in the name of "waiting on God," people fail to take responsibility or action. They wait for God to perform a miracle while God waits for them to act. Remember, we call them "miracles" because they rarely happen.

It is often easier to wait on a miracle than to do the difficult thing and take action. But unless we take action today, the pain will still be there or the person will still be involved with the destructive behavior tomorrow.

God wants our faith to be active. That is a huge aspect of healthy balance! As we develop an active faith, our relationship with God is stretched, especially during those uncomfortable times when we must act beyond our comfort zones. These painful seasons make us more reliant on God. We seek his comfort and strength as we strive to accomplish those things we would rather avoid. Each risk we take brings us closer to God and builds our faith.

I met a couple who loved their son very much, even though he had disgraced them repeatedly with his drinking and drug use. There seemed to be no end to the agony they went through for him. But instead of making him face his responsibilities, they paid his way and made life "safe" for him. They prayed that God would heal him of his affliction. They thought it was their job to support him while God worked on the addiction. One night in a drunken stupor, their son walked off a balcony and was killed. Those parents had to live with the guilt of knowing they never did anything to help. They only enabled his negative behavior as they waited for God to perform a miracle. Out of a toxic faith in God, they loved their son to death.

I also know of a wife who let her husband's unfaithfulness go unchecked. She knew he was running around, but she fervently prayed that God would change him. When she came down with a sexually transmitted disease, she knew the cause. Her husband left her with a "gift" that cannot be cured. If she had taken action, she could have spared herself a lifetime disease and perhaps saved her marriage.

The Bible makes many references, especially in the Psalms, to waiting on the Lord. Some people have misinterpreted waiting on the Lord as a call to roll over and play dead. Hear me, please: *Waiting on the Lord does not mean turning off your brain.* Waiting on the Lord is waiting on God's timing and power. It means doing all we can in faith and turning over what we cannot do to the Lord. If we are unemployed, we should not use waiting on the Lord as an excuse to sit idly by and wait for a job to magically appear. God wants us to look for a job and go through interviews, all the while remembering that God is still God and we must wait on him.

Waiting on God for help does not mean we should turn off the mind he gave us or put to bed the body he formed for us. We must take action and do those things that we have the power and faith to do, then trust God to do those things that are not within our power and faith. This balanced approach will accomplish much without compelling us to do everything by ourselves. God gave us all many strengths. He expects us to use those strengths even while we depend on his strength to assist us.

THE IMBALANCE OF LAZINESS

Laziness is yet another imbalance that comes from an unhealthy faith. Many of us tend to dump responsibility for our lives on God. Rather than work to heal a marriage, for example, we want God to fix it instantly. Rather than make an appointment with a counselor, we pray for a miracle, asking God to do for us what God probably wants us to do for ourselves. It is inconvenient to go to a marriage counselor. It is expensive too. So rather than do the responsible thing, the lazy among us believe that if we just pray, God will take care of our marriage. Marriage counseling is a painful growth process. And yet God may want us to go through it.

One of the first illustrations I heard about the balance between taking action and being lazy involved two girls on their way to school. The moment for the bell to ring grew closer and closer. They had been late several times, and there would be grave consequences if they repeated the offense. One girl suggested they crawl down into the nearest ditch to pray to God that they would not be late. The other girl made the more realistic suggestion: they should pray and run!

Thousands of lazy believers have crawled down into ditches of unreality. They have retreated into a lazy world where they want everything worked out for them in a magical, mysterious way. They want a servant god; they don't want to serve God. They want a god drug that will wipe out consequences and quickly ease all hurts.

I think God might be watching, hoping they will crawl out of the ditches and continue to grow by facing their difficulties one at a time.

No Longer Infants

Healthy faith does not gravitate to one extreme or the other, nor does it oscillate between extremes. It seeks to be balanced in its expression. As our faith matures, "we will no longer be infants, tossed back and forth by the waves, and blown here and there by every wind of teaching and by the cunning and craftiness of men in their deceitful scheming" (Ephesians 4:14).

Total dedication to the cause of Christ does not necessitate irrational or wild-eyed behavior; in fact, it produces a calm life that blesses everyone it touches. As Paul wrote, "Make it your ambition to lead a quiet life, to mind your own business and to work with your hands, just as we told you, so that your daily life may win the respect of outsiders and so that you will not be dependent on anybody" (1 Thessalonians 4:11-12).

That sounds like balance to me—and it is a beauty to behold!

CHAPTER 16

THE TRADEMARK
OF HEAVEN

A Healthy Faith Is Loving

The commandments, "Do not commit adultery," "Do not murder," "Do
not steal," "Do not covet," and whatever other commandment there may
be, are summed up in this one rule: "Love your neighbor as yourself."

Romans 13:9

It has always disturbed me to see street-corner preachers yelling at people
about God. Certainly some men and women have come to Christ thanks
in part to such shouting and verbal abuse, but I believe that for every person who has been won to Christ, ten may have been alienated and even
humiliated.

Frankly, it doesn't seem very loving to me. And if it irritates me, I can
only imagine how it must provoke non-Christians.

Recently I heard of a new movement afoot that I find to be a loving,
caring alternative to street-corner bullhorns. It is meeting the need of thousands of people, showing them authentic love from the Father rather than
an obnoxious display of religiosity. The movement promotes what it calls
"prayer stations." Someone got the idea of setting up card tables on street

corners and in front of department stores where passersby can sit down and pray with a concerned believer.

What a great idea! If we have fortune-tellers and even massage therapists setting up shop on the street, why not prayer stations? It's such a wonderful twist on street-corner preaching. We've gone from yelling at people to praying for them when and where they're hurting. And the movement is growing. I love it!

THE CENTRAL THEME OF CHRISTIANITY

Love is the predominant characteristic of a healthy faith. And Christian love is not a warm, fuzzy feeling but a demonstration of care and concern for the well-being of another. True love is an extremely healing force. It values persons for who they are rather than for what they are able to do, and it enables believers to love God, themselves, and others. Those who experience genuine love are free to love others in the same freeing manner. Love creates positive emotional and spiritual bonds without equal.

Love is the central theme of Christianity. Christ demonstrated his love when he gave his life for us on the cross. In fact, what Jesus did for us on the cross gave us a new definition for love. "This is love," wrote John, "not that we loved God, but that he loved us and sent his Son as an atoning sacrifice for our sins" (1 John 4:10). He sacrificed himself not because of anything we did, not because we deserved it, but because he loved us just as we are.

Healthy believers reflect their Savior and therefore are full of love. Their love heals and helps them bear up under every trial. It is the foundation for an eternal future with God and for growing relationships with others. If believers have all the talents in the world, but do not have a deep and abiding love, their faith is worthless. But where love is present, faith grows, and people are attracted to God.

For good reason Paul told us, "The entire law is summed up in a single command: 'Love your neighbor as yourself'" (Galatians 5:14), and "Now

these three remain: faith, hope and love. But the greatest of these is love"
(1 Corinthians 13:13). No wonder the writer to the Hebrews said, "And let
us consider how we may spur one another on toward love and good deeds"
(Hebrews 10:24). And it makes sense that Peter would write, "Finally, all of
you, live in harmony with one another; be sympathetic, love as brothers, be
compassionate and humble" (1 Peter 3:8). Love is the hallmark of an authentic faith.

BUT WHAT IS LOVE?

According to the Bible's "love chapter," 1 Corinthians 13, love doesn't keep
track of how it has been mistreated. It keeps no record of wrongs. It does not
rejoice in evil but exults in the truth. It always protects, always trusts, always
hopes, always perseveres. It doesn't enable or endorse sinful behavior, but it
recognizes that we're all working out our faith in Jesus Christ. It enables us to
say to a fellow struggler, "I love you enough to stand with you as God works
in you."

The exercise of healthy faith allows a person to be *patient*, to trust that
God will not abandon or reject the one who sincerely comes to him. Healthy
believers are patient with others and themselves as they allow God to correct
their character defects. Such patience is seen only in the hearts of the healthy
faithful. If our faith does not move us to patience, it is not healthy.

Healthy faith also produces *kindness* toward others as we mature in love.
Healthy believers are also kind to themselves and find no need to punish
themselves when they miss the mark. This kindness is so attractive that others come to the faith because of it.

The love of healthy faith is also *humble*. When our focus is totally on
God, there is no room for pride. Neither is there rejection or rudeness or self-
seeking. Forgiveness is offered freely, for grudges and healthy faith cannot
coexist.

Healthy believers love, support, and accept one another. They lovingly assist those who want to cultivate a new relationship with God and his Son. They do not reject anyone because of differing beliefs, but they patiently work with all in a mutual search for truth. Healthy believers allow a person to be different and to make mistakes without being shamed. In short, the healthy believer is able to exemplify the characteristics outlined in the Bible's "love chapter."

HARD TO LIVE OUT

We all know 1 Corinthians 13 clearly describes love. But we also know true love is terribly hard to live out! I have great difficulty being patient and kind. I don't always refrain from envying or boasting or being rude or self-seeking. I struggle to always protect, always trust, always hope, always persevere. When I'm the object of someone's contempt, it is hard to look past his or her behavior to the brokenness behind it. In all candor, it is exceedingly difficult to practice what I preach!

I'm humbled by how easy it is to vilify the person with whom I'm in conflict, rather than take responsibility for what I may have contributed to the dispute. It's hard to acknowledge that I didn't set a boundary or wasn't as patient or as kind as I demanded that individual be of me.

And yet the nature of love doesn't change, for it is fixed forever by the nature of God, the Great Lover himself. Jesus reminds us of the unconditional, giving nature of divine love in his famous story of the Good Samaritan (Luke 10:30-37). There we see a priest pass by a Jewish man who had been robbed, stripped, beaten, and left half-dead. We see a Levite do the same thing. But a Samaritan—a hated half-breed—arrives on the scene and, acting with compassion, helps the wounded man. The stranger picked up the man, dressed his wounds, and gently put him on his own donkey. He didn't look into the man's background, he didn't ask if he were a homosexual, if he drank, or if he did drugs. There were no criteria for his love. He served the man as

Jesus would have. He took him to an inn, left his MasterCard, and said, "Whatever this guy needs, put it on my bill."

Jesus' parable is all about love, a kind of self-giving, unconditional love that issues from the very heart of God. I wonder how many of us have that kind of love for our fellowman.

MATURE VERSUS IMMATURE LOVE

Maybe our main problem is not that we lack love, but that our love isn't mature. For example, I know my daughter loves me [Jack], but it's an immature love. She's not able to empathize with me, to recognize that if we don't go to Disneyland on Saturday as I promised, it might be because I'm sick. It's that kind of immature love that can contaminate the church. We're often not mature enough to look at the brokenness behind an individual's sinful behavior, to be humble and empathize with those who are struggling.

An immature love is a needy form of love. It needs the constant approval of others to feel good about itself. An immature love says, "I have to perform to win the approval of others and even of God. I have to prove my worth to myself or to my pastor or to my world."

Mature love has no need to prove anything. It's a settled acceptance, a state of being. A mature love says, "God loves me. He may approve or disapprove of what I do, but that's not the same thing as approving or disapproving of who I am. That was settled long ago; it's unshakable. God loves me, period."

A mature love doesn't insist on having its own way. It is altruistic. It doesn't need someone to affirm that it's being loving in order to avoid getting angry. For example, I don't need my daughter to say to me, "Daddy, thank you for saying no to me because I know that you're loving me." I don't need for my clients to say, "Thank you, Therapist Jack, for confronting me with my immaturity and helping me to grow strong." A mature love refuses to lash out when it is hurt, and it continues to act for the well-being of others even when those others are trying to inflict pain on it.

As I think about this, I realize it must be terribly difficult to be a pastor's wife. They have to listen to a lot of griping from church people, and sometimes the criticism can cut pretty close to the bone. I know a pastor's wife who does a masterful job of handling personal attacks on her husband. Jill is able to hear them as expressions of the critic's struggle and not merely as an attack on her dearly loved spouse. She rarely gets defensive. She is able to empathize and say, "Well, if you're hearing it that way, it must be really hard for you. You ought to talk to Jim and sit down and find out if that's where he's coming from. As Jim's wife, I certainly experience him as patient and loving." She never seems to get upset with someone who is angry with her husband or with the church.

Once a woman in the church felt rejected by Jim and falsely accused him of sexual impropriety. It was obvious the charges could not be true, because Jim was known to be in another location when the alleged offense took place. Jill was frustrated with the hateful accusations, but still she was able to comfort this woman. How? Because she knew this woman was mentally ill, not spiritually rebellious. Even though the woman was making horrendous accusations about Jill's husband and trying to bring down the church, Jill felt sorry that she couldn't experience the love and security of God.

It's hard to comfort the person who's attacking your husband, but Jill did it. She illustrates for me that the greater empathy we show, the greater maturity we have. Without question, Jill is a woman of mature Christian love.

FROM IMMATURE TO MATURE LOVE

But how do you move a person from immature to mature love? What must happen for us to leave behind childish ways and embrace spiritual adulthood? There's only one way: by exposing the immature person to mature love without enabling the person's sin. That's a test for anybody! But God calls us to model a maturity that the immature lack.

For example, if I am the dad, I'm the one who's supposed to adapt. I'm supposed to be the mature one. But if I get angry with my little daughter for being upset—if I get mad at her because she's mad at me—then something is wrong with this picture. My immature daughter learns about mature love by watching me not getting upset. "I know you're upset with me," I might say. "I know you don't like me right now, and I know you think I'm being mean. But, no, you're not having your ice cream before dinner."

The immature learn about mature love only when they see it holding them accountable for their inappropriate behavior. They will never learn if we react with anger and condemnation, saying, in effect, "I'll love you when you're behaving right, but I won't love you when you're not behaving right." If we're unwilling to be present in someone's pain or rebellion, how will they ever learn what mature love is?

When I [Steve] think of a person who embodies mature Christian love, I think of my grandmother. She accepted people where they were, although she expected them to go beyond this. She had a servant's heart, but she put her foot down when my less-than-devoted grandfather wanted to run wild in Texas. While Mother Art expected great things from her family, she did not deny the reality of who her children or grandchildren were. She knew of our struggles and accepted us despite those struggles. And it didn't matter if it was the one who played football in the Sun Bowl or the one who just got out of jail. She was always there to give us hugs and kisses. Her home was always safe.

Mother Art felt it was her job to love people; it was our job to get our act together. And whether we were on top of the world spiritually or at the bottom, we always knew there was a place to heal at Grandma's house. We knew we'd find there a refuge where we could be accepted and loved, not lectured, not judged, but a home where we would be free to recuperate and mend.

When my first wife left me and I lost all my friends and my vision for my life, it was at Mother Art's place that I was able to regain my strength and equilibrium. When other members of my family visited me, I started hearing the lectures and the verses and all the sermons I didn't want to hear. That only depressed me. But because my grandmother was filled with mature Christian love, she knew just what I needed. Sometimes that was wise theology, but more often it was just a hug or a cup of hot tea.

A GREAT PARADOX

The more mature we become in our love, the more we realize how immature we really are. I [Jack] think it was Abraham Lincoln who said a man is no stronger than when he is able to admit his weaknesses. Only a mature love is able to work with such a paradox. I can be a mature person only when I am able to own my weaknesses. My daughter cannot say she is immature. A sign of her maturity will be when she is able to recognize her immaturity. That paradox is challenging!

I have to be able to look first at me. Am I being patient? Am I demanding from this person what I'm unwilling to give? In recent days I have had to ask myself those questions many times.

Chemotherapy makes one tired and grumpy, and I'm in the middle of it right now. Just the other night my wife, Robin, began talking to me about painting the front door. I snapped at her because I thought she didn't recognize I was sick and tired. She calmly replied, "Don't be so grumpy. I just asked you when you were going to paint it. I'm not disappointed because you're not painting it right now." And I had to say, "You know, you're right. I apologize. I'm tired and grumpy and I need a time-out."

As simple as that sounds, it's hard to do. It's easier to stay angry and make the other person the bad guy. I wanted to make the incident about Robin or my kids, rather than that I was sick and grumpy and needed a time-out. It takes a mature love to react with grace when you really want to take a swipe at someone's nose. And truth be told, none of us exhibit mature love all the time. That's the paradox: The more mature in love we become, the more we realize how immature we really are. There's always room for growth!

GOD IS LOVE

Why does the Bible insist that God's people act in love? It's simple, really. We are to reflect our Father, and God is love. Stop and think about that for a moment. Does the Bible say God is joy? Does the Bible say God is fear? Does the Bible say God is peace? No, it makes none of those claims. But it does say, "God is love" (1 John 4:8,16). If you believe in God, the true God, then you must believe in the love of God, because that is what he is. God is love.

Nor does the Bible say God is love for everyone but you. You are included among those whom God loves. The Bible does not say God loves only those who are perfect (or pretty close to it). No, God loves you and me even though we are far from perfect and far from being all we could be.

It is terribly sad how many Christians know intellectually that God loves them but don't experience him as a loving Father. Many Christians experience God as a provider, as an answerer of prayer, and as a disciplinarian, but not as a gentle Father whose heart breaks over their sins, who comforts them in their trials and tribulations.

Many Christians live in an unbiblical fear of a stern and punishing God. They fear that because of something they did or didn't do, God is going to punish them, destroy them, cast them into outer darkness. They do not see that even when God disciplines his children, it is because he loves them and wants to see them transformed into the image of Christ (see Hebrews 12:1-13). The wrath of God is not some uncontrolled, emotional rage that we suffer because we embarrass him.

It is crucial to recognize that a healthy relationship with God is based on love, not on fear of reprisal. A sense of impending doom will ultimately lead to a fruitless life and a sense of alienation from God, while a love-based relationship will lead to communion with God and a fruitful spiritual life. Those who enjoy a love-based relationship with God have a much easier time being patient, kind, gentle, loving, and self-controlled with those who might be living in sin or in rebellion against God. Fear-based Christians often become intolerant, Bible-thumping, unkind, cruel, shaming, condescending, hard, bitter, and unable to control their tongue or their temper.

Love is a much stronger and more enduring motivator than fear. For example, what keeps a godly man from having an affair? Not the fear that his wife will leave him if he does, but a deep love for her that recoils at the thought of causing such awful pain. If mature human love is like that, think how much more committed God is to loving us! How much more, then, should our relationship with him be love-based and not fear-based!

When we forget that God is love, we often slide toward methods and practices like those of the pastor of a small church in southern California, a little man who saw himself in a big way. He wanted total control over his congregation and his members allowed him to have it. The control was often negative and punitive.

One day an unmarried woman told the pastor she had been involved in an affair with a married man in the church. She felt terrible about it and had broken off the relationship. She felt guilty and wanted to confess her sin to the minister and receive his help in moving back to a close relationship with God.

The pastor was willing to help, but only if she would agree to some stressful conditions. He forced her to go to the man's wife and confess the sin to her. He forced her to go before the congregation and confess her sin before them. He forced her to agree not to date for one year as a sign of true contrition. Rather than offer her hope and a way back to her relationship with God, he offered her a set of difficult hoops to jump through—and those hoops eventually destroyed her.

Contrast that to Christ's approach when confronted with the adulterous woman (see John 8:1-11). He told her accusers to search themselves; any one of them who was free from sin could start the stoning. Not a single man so much as twitched, until one by one they all slunk away. At last Jesus turned to the woman. He did not provide a punitive system for her, but instead simply said to her, "Go now and leave your life of sin." Through Jesus, the woman felt the compassion of God, not his wrath.

It is imperative that we experience the love of God, that we might truly be able to restore those who are lost in sin, and that we do so with a spirit of gentleness rather than a spirit of condemnation. Our loving relationship with God enables us to become bright lanterns illuminating the path to God.

God is hung up on love, and out of his infinite love, Jesus Christ hung upon a cross. For us! It wouldn't be too much to paraphrase John 3:16 like this:

> For God was so hung up on love for us that his one-and-only
> Son hung upon a cross, that if any of us would give our hang-
> ups to him, we might hang out with him forever.

Okay, so it's not going to win any translation awards. But that's not the point! The point is, God is love, and because that's true, we can love too.

And that changes everything.

LIFE'S GREATEST PURSUIT

When all is said and done, what makes faith healthy? In my opinion, it comes down to honesty and integrity of the heart. Healthy faith uses Scripture to challenge itself, not justify itself. It is willing to be humbled, to surrender, to be held accountable, to be corrected, to be malleable in Christ's strong but gentle hands. It recognizes that God uses life experiences to do the hard work of transforming us into the image of his Son. So when we go through trials and tribulations, we know God is molding us into something beautiful, not persecuting us because of some wrongdoing or shortcoming in our character.

Developing a healthy faith in God is the greatest pursuit of a lifetime. It is a never-ending process with seasons of tremendous growth and times of near stagnation. At times God seems to direct every step we take, and at other times he feels as distant as another solar system.

Through every season he asks us to seek him as he seeks us. As we trust him more, our eyes and our hearts are opened to ever deeper chambers of his love and acceptance. He desires for us to grow and is lovingly tolerant of us even when we stubbornly refuse to do so. He is always there for us, and those with a healthy faith return to him quickly whenever they stray into sin.

A few years ago I encountered a fascinating study on the nature of mature Christian faith.[1] At least eight core elements characterize the one who has developed such a mature faith:

1. Trusts in God's saving grace and believes firmly in the humanity and divinity of Jesus.
2. Experiences a sense of personal well-being, security, and peace.
3. Integrates faith and life, seeing work, family, social relationships, and political choices as part of one's religious life.
4. Seeks spiritual growth through study, reflection, prayer, and discussion with others.
5. Seeks to be part of a community of believers in which people give witness to their faith and support and nourish one another.
6. Holds life-affirming values, including commitment to racial and gender equality, affirmation of cultural and religious diversity, and a personal sense of responsibility for the welfare of others.
7. Advocates social and global change to bring about greater social justice.
8. Serves humanity consistently and passionately through acts of love and justice.

Quite a list, isn't it? Just imagine how our world would change if all of us who claim the name of Christ could truly be said to possess a mature Christian faith. We'd change the world!

And why not? If first-century Christians were said to have turned the world upside down (Acts 17:6), why not twenty-first-century Christians? If those early believers could learn to mature and grow and manifest to their world a strong, healthy faith, why not us?

I pray that you will grow strong in your faith. I hope that you will find God to be your source of fulfillment. I encourage you to consider the words of Paul in 1 Corinthians 16:13-14: "Keep your eyes open for spiritual danger; stand true to the Lord; act like men; be strong; and whatever you do, do it with kindness and love" (TLB).

God loves you and wants you for his own. The more you give of yourself to him, the more joy you will have.

God bless you on your journey of faith as you seek to know God as he is.

NOTES

INTRODUCTION

1. Terry C. Muck, "Salt Substitutes—Grassroots Gullibility for Spiritual Counterfeits Demonstrates a Great Hunger for Things of the Spirit," *Christianity Today,* February 3, 1989, 14.

CHAPTER 3

1. Tiffany Potter, "A Mother's Love" in "Seniors and Their Inspirational Mentors," *The Orange County Register,* June 27, 1999.

CHAPTER 11

1. From Leslie B. Flynn, *Great Church Fights* (Wheaton: Victor, 1976), 105.

EPILOGUE

1. Peter L. Benson and Carolyn H. Eldin, *Effective Christian Education: A National Study of Protestant Congregations* (Minneapolis: Search Institute, 1990), 10.

Stephen Arterburn can be reached
by e-mail at sarterburn@newlife.com.

———

Jack Felton can be reached
by e-mail at jackfelton@jps.net.